POETRY PEOPLE

POETRY PEOPLE

A Practical Guide to Children's Poets

Sylvia M. Vardell

LIBRARIES UNLIMITED

A Member of the Greenwood Publishing Group

Westport, Connecticut • London

Library of Congress Cataloging-in-Publication Data

Vardell, Sylvia M.
Poetry people : a practical guide to children's poets / Sylvia M. Vardell.
        p.   cm.
    Includes bibliographical references and index.
    ISBN-13: 978–1–59158–443–8 (alk. paper)
    1. Children's poetry, American—Bio-bibliography—Dictionaries.   2. Children's
poetry, American—History and criticism.   3. American poetry—20th
century—Bio-bibliography—Dictionaries.   4. Poets, American—20th
century—Biography—Dictionaries.   I. Title.
    PS309.C48V37   2007
    811′.6099282–dc22   2007003329

British Library Cataloguing in Publication Data is available.

Library of Congress Catalog Card Number: 2007003329
ISBN-13: 978-1-59158-443-8

First published in 2007

Libraries Unlimited, 88 Post Road West, Westport, CT 06881
A Member of the Greenwood Publishing Group, Inc.
www.lu.com

Printed in the United States of America

The paper used in this book complies with the
Permanent Paper Standard issued by the National
Information Standards Organization (Z39.48–1984).

10 9 8 7 6 5 4 3 2 1

Contents

Acknowledgments

I am so grateful for the support of many people in bringing this project from idea to reality. My heartfelt thanks to the graduate students and graduate assistants who diligently assisted with research and bibliographic support: Mu-Chia Chen, Margie Daniels, Sarah Gosselink, Barbara Katz, Lola Ellen Buchanan, and Ann Sloan; my understanding editor at Libraries Unlimited, Sharon Coatney; and my supportive family: my endlessly patient husband, Russell Vardell, encouraging children, Alex and Emily, and helpful mom, Ingrid Mergeler. I'd also like to thank the poets themselves, many of whom responded to requests for additional information and input with such kindness and enthusiasm. Lee Bennett Hopkins and Marilyn Singer were particularly generous in answering every query throughout this journey. Thank you all.

Introduction

Next to being a great poet is the power of understanding one.
—Henry Wadsworth Longfellow

We are experiencing a renaissance in children's poetry publishing in recent years with greater interest in poets, poetry books, poetry jams and slams, poetry Web sites, National Poetry Month, etc. What is it about life's big and little moments that calls for a poem? On greeting cards. In a toast at a wedding. At moments of great happiness or deep sadness. Poems are short and full of interesting language, but it is the emotion or experience in a nutshell that gives poetry its power.

Poetry is a rich literary tradition that has stood the test of time from nursery rhymes to classic epics and provides a shared experience that brings adults and children together—to read aloud, listen to, and talk about. It provides a social connection as well as a language experience that helps children move forward in their literacy development. Mem Fox, author and literacy expert, says, "Rhymers will be readers; it's that simple. Experts in literacy and child development have discovered that if children know eight nursery rhymes by heart by the time they're four years old, they're usually among the best readers by the time they're eight" (2001, p. 85). Poetry has value for any of us at any age, but for children who are growing in their knowledge of language and literature, poetry is essential for their developing minds and hearts.

Why is there such apathy or resistance when the topic of poetry comes up? Even the word "poetry" reminds many people of forced memorization, searching for hidden symbolism, or counting for meter. So many adults have had negative experiences with poetry in the past that it keeps them from sharing poetry with children. Children then grow into a similar dislike or apathy for poetry. Findings from a recent study by the Poetry Foundation found that a lifelong love for poetry is most likely if cultivated early in childhood. How do we break the cycle of apathy and change negative attitudes? By getting to know new poets and their work.

The purpose of this book is to provide a comprehensive introduction to a variety of wonderful poets writing for young people. The book focuses primarily on contemporary poets who are still actively writing today, including poets appropriate for children ages 5–12. The featured poets are known predominantly for specializing in writing poetry for children and they include major award winners, popular bestsellers, and multicultural voices.

There is one entry for each of the sixty-two poets featuring brief biographical information, highlighting selected poetry books and poems they've authored, showcasing awards won, noting related Web sites, connecting relevant fiction and nonfiction titles, linking with other poets and poetry, and providing suggestions for programming activities. Poetry books unfortunately go out of print so quickly, so many titles cited may no longer be in print. However, many individual poems highlighted will be available in current anthologies as well as in single collections of poetry. And the recommendations here are only a beginning once one discovers favorite poets and poetry to share. This book is intended to be a practical guide for librarians and others who want to capitalize on the growing celebration of National Poetry Month and Young People's Poetry Week (both in April), as well as other occasions that call for poetry. Typically, most adults are familiar with adult poets and rely on their rusty memories for the names of noteworthy poets: Robert Louis Stevenson, Emily Dickinson, Robert Frost, etc. But when it comes to knowing today's children's poets, many adults think of Shel Silverstein and Jack Prelutsky, and then draw a blank. Most are probably not aware that there are so many poets writing for young people today. This guide offers enough material to feature a poet a week, if desired, focusing on current works and known standards that are very likely on the library's shelves right now.

Additional information is also provided to supplement the poet profiles. This includes a docket of poets to watch who are relatively new to the field, a roster of established fiction and nonfiction authors who also write poetry, and lists of verse novelists, anthologists, and classic poets from bygone eras. A catalog of awards for children's poetry is also provided, as is a roll call of helpful poetry Web sites, a list of poems about libraries and reading, a resource of poet biographies, autobiographies and memoirs, recommendations of must-have poetry anthologies, a poetry practices checklist, and tips for poet promotion activities. A calendar of poet birthdays month by month can assist with planning poetry celebrations, too. It is hoped that librarians, teachers, and others who serve children and young adults will find this a helpful resource for sharing more poetry with children in creative ways. We need to provide children with a bridge from the Mother Goose rhymes of preschool to the classic poems they will likely encounter in high school, college and beyond. How does that happen? By sharing these unique voices who are dedicated to writing poetry especially for children.

Arnold Adoff

http://www.arnoldadoff.com/

ARNOLD ADOFF'S BIO

Arnold Adoff was born on July 16, 1935, in New York City, and received his bachelor's degree from the City College of New York. He was a teacher in the New York City public school system and later served as a lecturer and consultant for several other federal projects and educational institutions. Throughout his career he has worked as a poet, anthologist, and writer of fiction and nonfiction and emerged as one of the first advocates of multiculturalism in American children's literature. In particular, he created several landmark anthologies of African American poetry for young people that are a staple of many library collections. Arnold Adoff was married to the distinguished children's book author Virginia Hamilton, and has a son, Jaime Adoff, who is also a writer and poet.

In 1988, Arnold Adoff became the eighth winner of the Award for Excellence in Poetry for Children given by the National Council of Teachers of English to honor a living American poet for his or her lifetime achievement in works for children ages 3–13. His individual poetry books have also received many other recognitions including citations as: *School Library Journal* Best Book, NCSS/CBC Notable Children's Trade Book, IRA Children's Choice, New York Public Library Books for the Teen Age, Parents' Choice Award, ALA Notable Book, and ALA Best Books for Young Adults.

ARNOLD ADOFF'S POETRY

Arnold Adoff has created both well-regarded anthologies as well as distinctive collections of original poetry on a variety of topics. Adoff has edited at least eight major anthologies of poetry and stories by African American writers within his body of 30 or more works. Begin with two of these that are particularly engaging for children, *I am the Darker Brother: An Anthology of Modern Poems by Negro Americans* first published in 1968 (reprinted by Simon & Schuster, 1997) and *My Black Me: A Beginning Book of Black Poetry* (Dutton, 1974). Children may recognize some of the most famous African American poets ever like Langston Hughes and enjoy encountering others who may be less familiar to them. These are names that are often hailed during Black History Month, so children can become familiar with Paul Laurence Dunbar, Countee Cullen, Lucille Clifton, Maya Angelou, and others through works that are selected specifically with young people in mind. Children can choose their favorite poem by one of these notable African American poets and look for a work of art by an African American artist like Jacob Lawrence, Clementine Hunter, William H. Johnson, and others to accompany it. For one outstanding example, look for *Words with Wings: A Treasury of African-American Poetry and Art* with masterworks of poems and paintings selected by Belinda Rochelle (HarperCollins, 2001).

Besides these noteworthy anthologies and others, Adoff has also created original poetry that explores the role of race in ordinary family life, often mirroring the experiences of his own biracial family. Pair these two picture book poem collections for sharing: *Black Is Brown Is Tan* (HarperCollins, 1973), often credited as being the first children's book to feature an interracial family, and *All the Colors of the Race* (Lothrop, Lee & Shepard, 1982), told from the point of view of a child with a black mother and a white father. Compare and contrast the points raised in each poetry book using a Venn diagram to show similarities and differences. Follow up with the picture book, *Two Mrs. Gibsons* by Toyomi Igus and illustrated by Daryl Wells (Children's Book Press, 1996). In this story, a young girl lovingly describes her African American grandmother and Japanese American mother, both called "Mrs. Gibson."

Adoff has also created more poetry on other everyday topics, such as sports and food. These are poems that often help woo some of the boys who think they don't like poetry (although many boys are poetry-lovers already, of course). They are often surprised to find that poets have written about basketball or running, for example. Check out Adoff's collections, *I Am the Running Girl* (HarperCollins, 1979), *Sports Pages* (Lippincott, 1986), or *The Basket Counts* (Simon & Schuster, 2000). Encourage the student athletes to share their stories or perhaps prepare their own read aloud of their favorite sports poems. Invite coaches to post sports poems in the gym or to visit as guest readers of sports poetry. Food is the subject of two of Arnold Adoff's other books, *Eats* (Lothrop, Lee & Shepard, 1979) and *Chocolate Dreams* (Lothrop, Lee & Shepard, 1988). Of course these poems can accompany an edible break with food to match the poem.

Adoff's poetry is noted for its creative use of capitalization and punctuation much like the work of e e cummings. Sometimes called "shaped speech," this use of space on the page helps create a distinctive rhythm in his poetry, which Adoff manipulates purposefully. Children often respond to it because it looks like he is "breaking the rules." Look for *Street Music: City Poems* (HarperCollins, 1995) or *Touch the Poem* (Scholastic, 1996) for fun, accessible poems that are spread out across the page in ways that invite kids to imitate and experiment. Pair Adoff's work with the poems of Nikki Giovanni, a noted poet who also uses rhythm, text, and spacing in distinctive ways. For cross-cultural connections look for *The Animals* by Michio Mado (McElderry, 1992) and contrast Mado's and Adoff's use of descriptive phrases to create images. This is also an excellent opportunity for using magnetic poetry and encouraging children to manipulate and spread out words and phrases to create poems in Adoff's visual style.

Francisco Xavier Alarcón

FRANCISCO XAVIER ALARCÓN'S BIO

Francisco Alarcón was born on February 21, 1954, in Wilmington, California and grew up in both California and Mexico. He received his Bachelor of Arts degree in Spanish and History from California State University, Long Beach, and a Master of Arts degree in contemporary Latin-American literature.

Alarcón has worked as a dishwasher, grape harvester, research assistant, summer youth counselor, translator, Spanish teacher, and a park ranger. He began writing poetry during his college years and draws upon his experiences in his neighborhood and from his heritage. Alarcón has received the American Book Award and several Pura Belpré Honor Awards, Parents' Choice awards, Tomás Rivera Mexican American award nominations, Americás Award Commendations, and American Library Association Notable citations, among others.

FRANCISCO X. ALARCÓN'S POETRY

Francisco Alarcón has written poetry for both children and adults, including bilingual collections in Spanish and English. His best-known work for young people is probably his series of four books focusing on the four seasons of the year, called *The Magical Cycle of the Seasons* series each illustrated in colorful, playful scenes by artist Maya Christina Gonzalez. Although each book can stand on its own, they make a lovely set of verses in Spanish and English for sharing throughout the year:

> SPRING: *Laughing Tomatoes and Other Spring Poems/ Jitomates Resuenos y Otros Poemas de Primavera.* (Children's Book Press, 1997)
>
> SUMMER: *From the Bellybutton of the Moon and Other Summer Poems/ Del Ombligo de la Luna y Otros Poemas de Verano.* (Children's Book Press, 1998)
>
> FALL: *Angels Ride Bikes: And Other Fall Poems/ Los Angeles Andan en Bicicleta: Y Otros Poemas de Otoño.* (Children's Book Press, 1999)
>
> WINTER: *Iguanas in the Snow/Iguanas en la nieve.* (Children's Book Press, 2001)

Each collection is full of autobiographical reminiscences that may prompt children to remember special moments in their own families or neighborhoods. Invite children to bring in a family photo of a favorite activity and sort these photos by seasons: spring, summer, fall, or winter. Children can then find or write poems to match the activities or seasons and post these together.

Each of Alarcón's picture book poetry collections is also worthy of sharing individually. In *Laughing Tomatoes and Other Spring Poems/Jitomates Resuenos y Otros Poemas de Primavera*, for example, his work is full of food imagery. Bring in samples of tomatoes and chiles to taste alongside the poems that describe them. In addition, many of Alarcón's poems can be read aloud by two voices. One voice reads the poem in English, another person reads the Spanish version, first individually, then simultaneously. Just be sure each person starts his/her line at the same time for the simultaneous reading. Here's one example.

Dew	*El Rocio*
the fresh	el fresco
taste	sabor
of the night	de la noche

When sharing Alarcón's *From the Bellybutton of the Moon and Other Summer Poems/Del Ombligo de la Luna y Otros Poemas de Verano*, invite children to talk about family trips they have taken or visits with extended family members. Find similar books about family gatherings to share on this topic like *Bigmama's* (Greenwillow, 1991) by Donald Crews or *The Relatives Came* by Cynthia Rylant (Atheneum, 1985). Link with family poems by Arnold Adoff such as *Black Is Brown Is Tan* (HarperCollins, 2002) or Mary Ann Hoberman's poetry in *Fathers, Mothers, Sisters, Brothers: A Collection of Family Poems* (Joy Street, 1991).

In *Angels Ride Bikes/Los Angeles Andan en Bicicleta* Alarcón celebrates simple events of everyday life that occur in the fall like the first day of school. And with *Iguanas in the Snow/Iguanas en la Nieve* the focus is on playful winter activities, including writing poetry. Invite the children to chronicle their year with poems about their own life experiences, particularly as they begin the school year and plan for fall holiday celebrations with family. Bring in Mary Lankford's nonfiction books for more information about traditions and celebrations around the world, such as *Christmas USA* (HarperCollins, 2006), *Hopscotch Around the World* (HarperCollins, 1992), and *Birthdays Around the World* (HarperCollins, 2002).

In his book *Poems to Dream Together/Poemas Para Soñar Juntos* (Lee and Low, 2005), Alarcón focuses again on family and community through bilingual poems about dreams and goals. For example, one poem honors the work of César Chávez. Others spotlight education, ecology, or peace. In addition, several of Alarcón's collections include footnotes with explanations for unfamiliar terms in Spanish and English. Challenge children to translate some of their poems into languages other than English. Invite guest readers, if needed, to read poems in other languages. Children may be surprised that many of Alarcón's poems rhyme in Spanish, but not in English. Why might that be? Talk with children about how translators must struggle with choosing only rhyming words to maintain the rhyme scheme, or sacrifice rhyme so that they can choose words that reflect the poem's meaning more closely. Follow up with poetry by other Latino and Latina poets who incorporate Spanish into their English poetry such as Gary Soto and Pat Mora.

Kathi Appelt

KATHI APPELT'S BIO

Kathi Appelt was born on July 6, 1954, in the front seat of her father's Ford. She grew up in Texas with two sisters, keeping a regular journal from a very young age. She is now married with two grown sons and draws much of her inspiration for writing from her own life experiences. She is also a teacher and mentor for other emerging authors and poets. Appelt is one of those rare authors who writes effectively for the very young as well as for the older teen. She has authored over 20 picture books for young people and half a dozen works for young adults. Although the language and phrasing of her picture books is often very lyrical, her poetry books are best suited to readers in the middle grades and above.

Kathi Appelt's work has been selected as an International Reading Association Teacher's Choice, an American Library Association Best Book for Young Adults, a New York Public Library Best Book of 1996, an American Library Association Quick Pick for Reluctant Readers, and by the Texas Library Association for the TAYSHAS List, among others.

KATHI APPELT'S POETRY

Kathi Appelt's poetry includes two collections with advice for aspiring poets: *Just People & Paper/Pen/Poem: A Young Writer's Way to Begin* (Absey & Co., 1997), *Poems from Homeroom: A Writer's Place to Start* (Holt, 2002). Each of these collections is divided into two sections, the first containing original free verse poems by Appelt herself and the second an exploration of the poem writing process along with strategies for writing original poetry. In particular, Appelt shares insider information on the crafting of each of her own poems and accompanies this with questions to prompt young readers to respond poetically themselves. She challenges readers to consider the motivation behind each poem and even invites them to experiment with different forms of poetry including the sestina, villanelle, and haiku. Each book is practical and pleasing, with a real heart for how young writers begin. Combine this pair with Paul Janeczko's *Seeing the Blue Between: Advice and Inspiration for Young Poets* (Candlewick, 2002) which follows a similar format, but includes the voices and advice of many different poets, or link with Naomi Shihab Nye's compilation of poetry written by children, *Salting the Ocean: 100 Poems by Young Poets* (Greenwillow, 2000).

Appelt reports that she uses a computer to write the text for her picture books and novels, but she uses a pencil and paper when she writes poetry because she says it forces her to slow down her thoughts, thus letting her catch the rhythm of a line. This may surprise young writers who value speed in their writing and pride themselves on typing quickly on a computer keyboard. Sometimes there is value in slowing the writing process down. Challenge children to compare these writing processes. Divide the group in half and allow one team to work on a computer and another to write with paper and pencil. They can try creating a simple formula poem like a list poem (I like, I wish, or Today I . . .) and then bring the two groups together to compare poems and processes.

For another application of Appelt's work, consider her poem "Homeroom" from *Poems from Homeroom: A Writer's Place to Start* (Holt, 2002). It is a thoughtful exploration of a possible definition of poetry. It begins, "Poetry is the home for all my yearnings/each poem a separate room/where wandering words/find a cool bed." Read and discuss the poem and encourage young writers to try creating their own poetic definition of what poetry is to them. Or look for other poems about poetry, such as "The Bridge" by Kaissar Afif from *The Space Between Our Footsteps* also collected by Naomi Shihab Nye (Simon & Schuster 1998).

Perhaps Appelt's most personal work is *My Father's Summers* (Holt, 2004), a compilation of prose poems and actual family photos from her own childhood and teen years. Although the context is her own growing up in the 1960s in Texas, the central conflict of the book is her own struggle with her parent's divorce and the divided life she must live thereafter. Appelt's pairing of poems and photos might inspire young poets to explore using their own photographs or magazine images to prompt their poem writing. Other books of poetry that incorporate photographs effectively include Karen Hesse's verse novel, *Witness* (Scholastic, 2001) and Lee Bennett Hopkins' autobiographical *Been to Yesterdays* (Wordsong/Boyds Mills Press, 1995). Look for Gary Soto's poem, "Ode to Family Photographs" from *Neighborhood Odes* (Harcourt, 1992) for a more light-hearted reminiscence of family times or the poetry picture books of Charles R. Smith such as *Perfect Harmony; A Musical Journey with the Boys Choir of Harlem* (Jump at the Sun/Hyperion, 2002) for a creative use of photo-collage and poetry. Children may want to create a scrapbook of photos and poems to document their own lives and experiences.

Brod Bagert

http://www.brodbagert.com

BROD BAGERT'S POETRY

Brod Bagert's work is characterized by a strong rhyme and rhythm that beg to be read aloud. In fact, many of his books are subtitled "poems to perform." Most are humorous, even hilarious and often from the child's point of view or in a child's voice. They lend themselves to a cheer or chant format for group or individual voices. Invite children to join in on reading aloud poems from the following collections:

* *Let Me Be the Boss: Poems for Kids to Perform* (Boyds Mills Press, 1992)
* *Chicken Socks and Other Contagious Poems* (Boyds Mills Press, 1993)
* *Elephant Games and Other Playful Poems to Perform* (Boyds Mills Press, 1995)
* *Gooch Machine: Poems for Children to Perform* (Boyds Mills Press, 1997)
* *Giant Children* (Dial, 2002)
* *Shout!* (Dial, 2007)

For example, the poem "Chocolate Maniac" from *Giant Children* lends itself to choral reading. Seven volunteers can each read aloud one stanza or you can break up the group into four subgroups and each subgroup reads one line of each stanza. (Each stanza has four lines.) Have a bowl of chocolate candy ready to sample after reading this poem. Perform this poem on October 28 to celebrate National Chocolate Day!

Bagert is a vocal advocate for poetry performance with children. In an essay, "Act It Out: Making Poetry Come Alive" which appeared in *Invitation To Read: More Children's Literature in the Reading Program* (International Reading Association, 1992), Bagert encouraged readers to become aware of how they can use their faces, voices, and bodies to perform poetry effectively. With modeling and practice each of these variables can be more consciously manipulated. He recommended: "Try this exercise. Make a sad face. Droop your eyes, pout your bottom lip, tilt your head to the side and say, 'I am not very happy.' You will find that voice, body, and timing tend to follow your expression. Now try to defy nature. Make the same sad expression and try to say, 'I am very happy' in a cheerful voice. You will find that it is very hard to sound happy when your face is sad. Conduct the search for what a poem means and how to perform it by asking a single question: *What face should I make when I say these words?* Then make the face and say the words." Try these steps with children; they really work. Bagert designs his poems to be performed with proper expression and intonation and with a bit of practice children catch on quickly. In fact, his outrageous humor and shout-out rhymes are nearly irresistible.

Pair Brod Bagert's writing with another poet whose writing begs to be performed, song and comedy writer, Alan Katz. His poems are "silly dilly" song rhymes set to familiar song tunes that most children will recognize. Poems such as "Take Me Out of the Bathtub" and "Go Go Go to Bed" are designed to be sung with gusto. In addition, relative newcomer, Kenn Nesbitt spins poems and songs in a similar vein, about subjects such as aliens, school, and Santa. Each of these writers offers poetry with an extra strong rhythm and tempo. They are the poetic equivalent of tall tales, taking humor and exaggeration to new levels. Children can choose their favorites to perform solo or in small groups; they can sing them accompanied with simple musical instruments, or add movement and gestures for emphasis.

Bagert has also authored a collection of poetry directed specifically at teachers and other school staff: *Rainbows, Head Lice, and Pea-Green Tile: Poems in the Voice of the Classroom Teacher* (Maupin House, 1999). These poems offer a wry examination of life at school. Librarians, in particular, may enjoy the poem "Library-Gold" about a reluctant reader who finds the just right book thanks to a helpful librarian. Contrast his poems about teaching with those by Cheryl Miller Thurston in *Hide Your Ex-lax under the Wheaties: Poems about Schools, Teachers, Kids, and Education* (Cottonwood Press, 1987). For poems about life at school from the child's perspective, look for the work of Kalli Dakos such as *If You're Not Here, Please Raise Your Hand* (Four Winds, 1990) or Carol Diggory Shields *Lunch Money and Other Poems about School* (Dutton, 1995). Kids can choose their favorite "school" poem to share during school programs, open houses, or morning announcements (with permission).

Calef Brown

http://www.calefbrown.com/

CALEF BROWN'S BIO

Calef Brown lives in California and graduated from the Art Center College of Design in Pasadena, California. He has worked as a freelance illustrator for magazines and newspapers and has also created art for book covers, CDs, and beverage cans. His paintings have been exhibited in New York, Los Angeles, San Francisco, Japan, and Italy. He travels regularly to Maine to write, paint, and create.

CALEF BROWN'S POETRY

Both an author and illustrator, Calef Brown's picture book poem collections are billed as "stories" and include vivid, curious paintings as well as rhythmic story poems: *Polkabats and Octopus Slacks: 14 Stories* (Houghton Mifflin, 1998) and *Dutch Sneakers and Flea Keepers: 14 More Stories* (Houghton Mifflin, 2000) and *Flamingos on the Roof* (Houghton Mifflin, 2006). His writing has often been compared to the nonsensical narratives of Edward Lear, so one must pull some of Lear's classic poetry, such as *The Owl and the Pussycat* illustrated by James Marshall (HarperCollins, 1998) for comparison. As we experiment with pairing individual poems together, sometimes a contemporary poem can offer a bridge to understanding an older, classic poem. Or for students who are already familiar with the classic poems, it can provide a basis for comparison and discussion. Another example is Laura E. Richards' classic poem, "Eletelephony," a natural partner to Calef Brown's poem, "Kansas City Octopus."

In fact, in Brown's first collection, *Polkabats and Octopus Slacks*, the opening poem, "Kansas City Octopus" imagines what an octopus might look like in "snazzy" new slacks. The accompanying painting helps visualize this unusual sight. Bring a sampling of fabric swatches like corduroy and invite the children to dress other animal characters they can imagine by creating an animal collage with fabric on paper. An ostrich in a dress? A bear in a bathing suit? Other poets who create inventive characters of all kinds with smart, clever language include J. Patrick Lewis (*A Hippopotamusn't and Other Animal Verses*, Dial, 1990), Kurt Cyrus (*Oddhopper Opera*, Harcourt Brace, 2001), X. J. Kennedy (*Ghastlies, Goops & Pincushions*, McElderry, 1989), Douglas Florian (*Monster Motel*, Harcourt, 1993), and Nancy Willard (*Pish, Posh, Said Hieronymus Bosch*, Harcourt, 1991).

Look for "The Runaway Waffle" in Calef Brown's second book, *Dutch Sneakers and Flea Keepers.* Here we see a waffle with arms and legs running away from a chasing girl. What other "runaway food" stories can the children think of? *The Gingerbread Man*? Or the classic *Journey Cake Ho* by Ruth Sawyer? Share and compare. Cut pieces of corrugated cardboard into circle shapes and give the children each a circle, pipe cleaners (for arms and legs) and markers or crayons to decorate their own runaway waffles.

Michael Cart in *Booklist* wrote "Welcome to *Tippintown*, where everything is a little bit weird—starting with the tour guide who has a blue face and an elephant's trunk for a nose." I can't decide which I enjoy more, Calef Brown's zany, syncopated story-poems or his crazy, cockeyed story-paintings that accompany his poetry. In this new collection of "poems and paintings" he invites us into his slightly askew worldview in which cats tango, dogs wear plaid, and people routinely have blue skin or blue hair. And his wordplay and strong rhythms build poems that stand on their own two (three or four) feet. My current favorite has got to be (picture the half caterpillar, half alligator creature in the illustration) "Allicatter Gatorpillar" from *Flamingos on the Roof* (Houghton Mifflin, 2006). This coining of a new creature by combining features of two animals into one is sure to inspire children to make their own creatures. Have the children draw pictures or cut magazine pictures to visualize their crazy animals. They may need help coining a new name by building a new word from two animal names. Follow up with Jack Prelutsky's similarly inventive poetry collection, *Behold the Brave Umbrelliphant* (Greenwillow, 2006). Share Brown's poetry books with children of all ages—read out loud for the fun of the words—and show the illustrations to inspire both your poets AND your painters.

Deborah Chandra

DEBORAH CHANDRA'S POETRY

Deborah Chandra's first work of poetry, *Balloons and Other Poems* (Farrar, Straus & Giroux, 1990) includes 24 poems about objects and experiences that will be familiar to most children, including a seashell, a goldfish in a pond, a cat's purr, and a piggyback ride. Many are so descriptive that it can be interesting to read the poem aloud *without* reading the title first and then encourage the children to guess the subject of the poem after hearing the poem details. In addition, bring the actual objects featured in the poems (a balloon, a seashell, a wrapped package, a pink rose, a sunflower, an autumn leaf) to show and display alongside the poems to make the images more concrete for children. Put the objects in a paper bag and invite a child to pull one object out—then read aloud the corresponding poem. Compare Chandra's poems with the free verse poems of Valerie Worth, which also lend themselves to object connections and guessing games.

In her second poetry collection, *Rich Lizard and Other Poems* (Farrar, Straus & Giroux, 1993), Chandra continues with 24 more poems about crickets, lizards, clouds, kites, cotton candy, and spider webs. The poem "Bubble" describes the experience of blowing bubbles through a plastic wand from a small container of soapy liquid—a childhood tradition. If it's possible to purchase or make individual bubble bottles for each child to use, that's the perfect accompaniment to the poem read aloud. And for libraries with a public statue, monument, or memorial nearby, Chandra's poem, "Statue in the Park" simply and beautifully describes a child's quiet encounter with a lady statue.

Read the poem outside near a local landmark. Bring paper and crayons to make a rubbing of the text on the historical marker at the statue, too.

Link Chandra's work with Rebecca Kai Dotlich's poetry (*Lemonade Sun and Other Summer Poems*, Wordsong/Boyds Mills, 1998) or Constance Levy's writing (*A Crack in the Clouds*, McElderry, 1998) to look at how poets use language to describe the everyday world. Contact a local museum of natural history or children's museum in the area to see if they have a "loan" program to borrow items (such as rocks, shells, animal skeletons, etc.) to pair and share with poems. Look for simple nonfiction books, such as the nature books of Jim Arnosky, the concept books of Tana Hoban, or the science picture books of Sandra Markle to supplement the poetry books with additional facts and photographs.

John Ciardi

JOHN CIARDI'S BIO

John Ciardi was born in Boston, Massachusetts, on June 24, 1916, and died in 1986. He received his bachelor's degree from Tufts College in 1938 and his master's degree in 1939 from the University of Michigan. He was also married and had three children. He was foremost a writer and a critic of adult poetry, but he also worked as a professor of English at several colleges and universities and then as poetry editor for *The Saturday Review*. He is probably best known for his well-regarded translation of Dante's *Inferno*. John Ciardi received many prestigious poetry awards during his long career including the NCTE Award for Excellence in Poetry for Children in 1982.

JOHN CIARDI'S POETRY

John Ciardi's poetry is known for its intelligence and sharp sense of comedy and irony. His first book, *The Reason for the Pelican* (Lippincott, 1959), had a major impact on the field of poetry for children, bringing in more irreverent humor and fun. And his poem "Mummy Slept Late while Daddy Cooked Breakfast" (from *You Read to Me, I'll Read to You*, HarperCollins, 1962/1987) is often listed as children's favorite poem in previous studies of children's poetry preferences. Although the poem assumes the stereotype that fathers don't know how to cook, it tells a humorous story about dad making a breakfast waffle that was in between "bituminous and anthracite" from the point of view of a child. Children can copy the Ciardi poem or create their own "breakfast" poems on paper placemats to take home and share. Follow up with a picture book about another family's busy morning, *Buzz* by Janet Wong (Harcourt, 2000).

Ciardi's collection, *You Read to Me, I'll Read to You* (Harper, 1962), is still in print after more than forty years. Much of today's contemporary humorous poetry for children owes a debt to John Ciardi. This collection of 35 poems includes directions for two readers to share reading the poems, the text and illustrations appearing in alternating colors of black and navy blue. Ciardi's irreverent poems are accompanied by Gorey's clever and offbeat illustrations. These smart rhymes and their zany picture partners helped to pave the way for Shel Silverstein, Jack Prelutsky, and even J. Patrick Lewis and Douglas Florian in the years to follow.

Another one of Ciardi's provocative poems, "Sometimes I Feel This Way" also from *You Read to Me, I'll Read to You* lends itself to a dramatic read aloud. It proposes we can choose to be "good" or "bad" each day by putting on the appropriate head and it features dialogue for two voices. Create a paper plate with a "be good" face on one side and a "be bad" face on the other for readers to hold up as they read their lines. Link this poem with the "Rotten Ralph" or "Joey Pigza" books by Jack Gantos about other characters struggling with good/bad behavior.

Ciardi's collection, *You Know Who* (Boyds Mills, 1991) includes the interestingly titled poem, "And Off He Went Just as Proud as You Please," a poem about names. This is a good poem to share at "get acquainted" times since it addresses how children often tease each other about their names. In this case, the names are merely "Billy" and "Willy" and thus there's irony in the teasing. Once again, this poem also lends itself to a two-reader dramatic reading (as do so many of Ciardi's poems for children) with one reader pretending to be Billy and another Willy. It may also lead to additional discussion about the variety of names children may encounter. Related books to share are *Chrysanthemum* by Kevin Henkes (Greenwillow, 1991), *The Name Jar* by Yangsook Choi (Knopf, 2001), or *My Name is Bilal* by Asma Mobin-Uddin (Boyds Mills Press, 2005).

John Ciardi lovingly skewers parent–child relationships in many of his collections. For example, *The Monster Den; Or, Look What Happened at My House—And to It* (Boyds Mills 1991) is a collection of humorous verse inspired by the author's family. His other notable anthologies include: *Someone Could Win a Polar Bear* (Boyds Mills Press, 2003), and *The Man Who Sang the Sillies* (HarperCollins, 1961), *Doodle Soup* (Houghton, 1985). Ciardi even has a compilation of 41 hilarious limericks illustrated by Susan Meddaugh, *The Hopeful Trout and Other Limericks* (Houghton Mifflin, 1992). Pair this with limericks by X. J. Kennedy (*Uncle Switch: Loony Limericks*, McElderry, 1997) and J. Patrick Lewis (*Boshblobberbosh: Runcible Poems for Edward Lear*, Creative Editions 1998) to model this distinctive five-line (AABBA) poem format for aspiring writers.

Kalli Dakos

http://www.kallidakos.com

KALLI DAKOS'S BIO

Kalli Dakos was born on June 16, 1950, in Ottawa, Canada. She received her bachelor's degree from Queen's University in Ontario and earned a master's degree from the University of Nevada, Reno. She studied journalism at Syracuse University in New York and worked briefly as a freelance writer for newspapers and magazines. She was an elementary school teacher and a reading specialist for nearly three decades. Dakos is married and has one daughter. Her work has twice been recognized with the Children's Choice Award.

KALLI DAKOS'S POETRY

The subject of school is the central focus of Kalli Dakos' poetry and children find the topic equally painful and hilarious through her work. In addition, Dakos employs a great variety of poetic forms and voices that lend themselves to varied choral performance techniques. Her school poems include:

If You're Not Here, Please Raise Your Hand (Four Winds Press, 1990)

(An unabridged audio version of this book is available from Recorded Books.)

Don't Read This Book, Whatever You Do! (Four Winds Press, 1993)

Mrs. Cole on an Onion Roll (Simon & Schuster, 1995)

The Goof Who Invented Homework (Dial, 1996)

The Bug in Teacher's Coffee (HarperCollins, 1999)

Put Your Eyes Up Here (Simon & Schuster, 2003)

Our Principal Promised to Kiss a Pig (Albert Whitman, 2004)

School is a favorite poetry topic to share with kids since it's where they spend so much of their waking hours. Dakos' collections can be the centerpiece for a school themed collection which could include these other poetry books about classroom life such as David Harrison's *Somebody Catch my Homework* (Wordsong Boyds Mills Press, 1993), *Almost Late to School and More School Poems* (Dutton, 2003) by Carol Diggory Shields, *I Thought I'd*

Take My Rat to School (Little, Brown, 1993) by Dorothy and X. J. Kennedy, or for older children, *The Dog Ate My Homework* by Sara Holbrook (Boyds Mills Press, 1997) and Helen Frost's *Spinning through the Universe: A Novel in Poems from Room 214* (Farrar, Straus & Giroux, 2004). Then link with Donald Crews' classic concept book, *School Bus* (Greenwillow, 1984) for a visual look at something familiar to students—the bus ride to school. Or for contrast, compare the contemporary poems with the historic view of school in *Forbidden Schoolhouse: The True and Dramatic Story of Prudence Crandall and Her Students* by Suzanne Jurmain (Houghton Mifflin, 2005).

Many of Dakos' poems express a strong point of view which makes them ideal for dramatic read aloud. For example, "I Brought a Worm" by Kalli Dakos from *If You're Not Here, Please Raise Your Hand* lends itself to a solo reading (along with a gummi worm prop!). Try "There's a Cobra in the Bathroom" by Kalli Dakos, with multiple parts for a teacher and several students who are seeking a missing (rubber) snake. Follow up with more snake poems like "The Boa" by Douglas Florian or "The Boa Constrictor" by Shel Silverstein. Seymour Simon's nonfiction book, *Snakes* (Collins, 2007), can provide excellent color photographs of actual snakes. Make worms or snakes out of clay or dough to display along with the poem.

Kalli Dakos' poem, "Call the Periods/Call the Commas" from *If Your Not Here, Please Raise Your Hand* is the perfect partner for Lynn Truss's picture book, *Eats, Shoots & Leaves* (Putnam, 2006). It's a clever picture book treatment of the difference a comma makes in everyday written language. Dakos' poem is arranged to suggest a breathless reading in dire need of punctuation. Together, they may lead to an interesting discussion of the place of punctuation in poetry as well as hilarious read aloud experiences.

The topic of the teacher has also been the focus of many of her poems. "But I Have Mr. Cratzbarg" by Kalli Dakos found in *Don't Read This Book, Whatever You Do*! or "Dancing on a Rainbow" from *If Your Not Here, Please Raise Your Hand* are both lovely tributes to those special teachers. Contrast these with Douglas Florian's "My Monster" poem from *Bing Bang Boing* (Harcourt, 1994), a more comic poem, and one that requires a sense of humor on the part of teachers. Use these poems to introduce any number of picture books about teachers such as *My Great Aunt Arizona* by Gloria Houston (HarperTrophy, 1997) or *The Teacher from the Black Lagoon* by Mike Thaler (Scholastic, 1989).

Dakos also has a wonderful poem about a librarian, "When the Librarian Reads to Us" from *Put Your Eyes Up Here: And Other School Poems*. In the three stanzas of this poem, Dakos uses strong rhythm and repetition to convey the "goose bumps" feeling children get from hearing good stories. It's a perfect poem to chant together or read aloud echo style, with the children repeating each line after the adult leader reads each line aloud. Gestures can be added for effect, shivering and rubbing their shaking arms every time the words "goose bump" are spoken. Make a poster of the poem with illustrations provided by the children themselves. Display it at the entrance to welcome guests to the library or in the read aloud area to use as an opening for group sessions.

Rebecca Kai Dotlich

http://www.rebeccakaidotlich.com/

REBECCA DOTLICH'S BIO

Rebecca Kai Dotlich was born on July 10 in Indianapolis, Indiana. She grew up in Indiana in the backyard of the Indy 500 and attended Indiana University. She began writing as a young child on a toy typewriter and eventually published her first collection of poetry for children, *Sweet Dreams of the Wild*, in 1995. She is a mother and grandmother, as well as a frequent conference speaker and writer-in-residence in the schools. In addition, she has been a poetry advisor for *Creative Classroom* magazine.

REBECCA DOTLICH'S POETRY

Rebecca Kai Dotlich has a particular talent for writing poetry for our youngest readers and listeners. With her book *Away We Go!* (HarperFestival, 2000), Dotlich introduces words, colors, and movements, in different simple forms of transportation. Once again, rhyming text along with the catchy phrase "Away we go!" will have listeners chanting along. Children can bring their favorite toy cars or trucks to line up and move as the poem's refrain is repeated.

Older children will enjoy her collection, *When Riddles Come Rumbling: Poems to Ponder* (Boyds Mills Press, 2001), a book of 29 poems describing everyday objects in riddle form. Here, the best approach is to read the rhyming puzzles out loud, talk about children's guesses with them, and then use the illustrations to figure out the solutions. Older readers will enjoy Dotlich's poetic picture book *What Is Science?* (Holt, 2006), an exploration of the field of science as well as the nature of scientific thinking. They may also enjoy digging up other books of riddles such as Brian Swann's riddle rhymes from African traditions (Browndeer Press, 1998) and Native American traditions (Browndeer Press, 1998) in his books, *The House with No Door* and *Touching the Distance.*

Other of Dotlich's works focus on family togetherness, including *Mama Loves* (HarperCollins, 2004) and *Grandpa Loves* (HarperCollins, 2005), two picture books describing a piglet "child's" relationship with his/her mother or grandfather. Each book offers a loving list of activities that characterize each figure—mother or grandfather. Children can pantomime the activities or discuss things they see their mothers, fathers, grandparents, or other caregivers doing. Follow up with Dotlich's *A Family Like Yours* (Boyds Mills

Press, 2002), a rhyming picture book that celebrates families. Link her family poems with those by Mary Ann Hoberman (*Fathers, Mothers, Sisters, Brothers: A Collection of Family Poems*, Little, Brown, 2001) or Ralph Fletcher (*Relatively Speaking*, Orchard, 1999) or with the family stories of Beverly Cleary or Grace Lin.

Dotlich has two collections that are full of movement, in their strong rhythms and in their content. *Over in the Pink House: New Jump Rope Rhymes* (Boyds Mills Press, 2004) includes 32 original rhymes for chanting aloud while jumping rope. With *In the Spin of Things: Poetry of Motion* (Boyds Mills Press, 2003), Dotlich finds movement in ordinary things like ice cubes, pencil sharpeners, etc. Both books are full of playfulness with words and actions. Combine them with Jane Yolen's *Street Rhymes Around the World* (Wordsong, 2003) and Joanna Cole's *Anna Banana: 101 Jump-Rope Rhymes* (HarperTrophy, 1989) for more playtime rhymes. Other jump-rope resources include *The Jump Rope Book* by Elizabeth Loredo and Martha Cooper (Workman, 1996), *Double Dutch: A Celebration of Jump Rope, Rhyme, and Sisterhood* by Veronica Chambers (Hyperion/Jump at the Sun, 2002). And of course, be prepared for spinning and jumping among the children and have the jump ropes ready.

At the other end of the activity spectrum is Dotlich's collection of bedtime poems, *Sweet Dreams of the Wild: Poems for Bedtime* (Boyds Mills Press, 1996). Here, sweet rhythmic poems describe how a variety of wild animals fall asleep. A repetitious opening invites child participation, much like *Brown Bear, Brown Bear* by Bill Martin, Jr. Share poems from this collection to help children wind down or prepare for naps or bedtime.

For preparing for summer or during summer gatherings, share Dotlich's *Lemonade Sun: And Other Summer Poems* (Boyds Mills Press, 1998). She captures childhood experiences with metaphorical language that focus on natural pleasures like enjoying butterflies and ladybugs, as well as games of jacks and jump rope. Once again, children will enjoy *doing* these summer activities or sharing incidents from their favorite summertime pastimes. Brainstorm a group list of favorites and encourage children to try new ones. Other summer poetry can be found in *July Is a Mad Mosquito* by J. Patrick Lewis (Atheneum, 1994), *Turtle in July* by Marilyn Singer (Macmillan, 1989), and *From the Bellybutton of the Moon and Other Summer Poems/ Del ombligo de la luna y otros poemas de verano* by Francisco X. Alarcón (Children's Book Press, 1998).

Dotlich also collaborated with fellow poet J. Patrick Lewis to write *Castles, Old Stone Poems* (Wordsong/Boyds Mills Press, 2006), an amazing tour of some of the world's most famous castle landmarks. Each of the 16 descriptive poems is presented in a beautifully illustrated double-page spread begging for discussing and locating each landmark on a world map. Additional endnotes and a timeline will guide the discussion. Follow up with sharing *Sacred Places* by Jane Yolen (Harcourt, 1996), a collection of poems about celebrated spiritual and cultural centers around the world or David Macaulay's classic picture book, *Castle* (Houghton Mifflin, 1977).

Barbara Juster Esbensen

http://www.ttinet.com/bje/writings.html

BARBARA ESBENSEN'S BIO

Barbara Esbensen was born on April 28, 1925, in Madison, Wisconsin, and graduated with a bachelor's degree from the University of Wisconsin in Madison. She worked as an art teacher for several years and as an advertising designer for a newspaper in Eureka, California briefly. Her interests included music and singing in a chorale group. She was married, had six children, and died in Minnesota in 1996.

Barbara Esbensen has won many awards including the NCTE Award for Excellence in Poetry for Children, the Lee Bennett Hopkins Poetry Award for her book *Dance with Me* (HarperCollins, 1995), and several notable citations by the American Library Association and the National Council of Teachers of English.

BARBARA ESBENSEN'S POETRY

Barbara Esbensen's poetry collections are strong in imagery, fresh perspective, and a deft use of language. Her focus on animals and nature is particularly appealing in such books as *Echoes for the Eye: Poems to Celebrate Patterns in Nature* (HarperCollins, 1996), *Who Shrank My Grandmother's House? Poems of Discovery* (HarperCollins, 1992), and *Words with Wrinkled Knees* (Crowell, 1986).

In the world of poetry, it's fairly unique to find examples of poems that support learning mathematics. But because much of mathematics deals with numbers, theories, and calculations, the language and imagery of poetry may help children visualize abstract concepts and operations. Esbensen's book *Echoes for the Eye: Poems to Celebrate Patterns in Nature* is one such unique example. It includes a study of shapes, patterns, or geometry, and the math in everyday life. Other books with math-related poems include Lee Bennett Hopkins' *Marvelous Math* (Simon & Schuster, 1997), Mary O'Neill's classic *Take a Number* (Doubleday, 1968), and Betsy Franco's *Mathematickles!* (Simon & Schuster, 2003). Children can bring in sets of objects such as buttons, pebbles, paperclips, leaves, etc., to count, organize in number sets, and match with their corresponding poems.

Esbensen has also authored both nature poems and nature nonfiction books which can be shared separately or in combination. Her poem collections, *Who Shrank My Grandmother's House? Poems of Discovery* and *Cold Stars and Fireflies* (Crowell, 1991) and *Swing Around the Sun* (Lerner, 2002) celebrate the seasons, the natural world, and the poet's curiosity about it all in lovely free verse poetry. Parallel her perspective with that of Joseph Bruchac in *Thirteen Moons on Turtle's Back: A Native American Year of Moons* (Philomel, 1992). Other nature poets with a similar style of writing include Constance Levy and Kristine O'Connell George. Contrast Esbensen's nature poetry with her poetic use of language in her nonfiction picture books, including:

Swift Is The Wind: The Cheetah (Orchard Books, 1996)

Great Northern Diver: The Loon (Little, Brown, 1990)

Tiger With Wings: The Great Horned Owl (Orchard, 1991)

Baby Whales Drink Milk (HarperCollins, 1994)

Esbensen's book, *Words with Wrinkled Knees*, is a creative exploration of both the *words* as well as *attributes* of animals and animal names. For example, she imagines the giraffe in the library with the phrases "this word/ munches on the leaves/ of books lined up" and portrays the dinosaur with "out-of-print/ bones." These library connections are especially fun and suggest activities such as posting animal poems near the animal books, looking for other places to connect with new animal creations, and creating new animal wordplays such as acrostics, crossword puzzles, and word scrambles.

There's nothing quite like seeing the rough drafts of a published poem. The finished product we read in a book seems so perfect that it's hard to imagine the writer ever struggling with every word and phrase. This is particularly true for children who think adults never make mistakes in their writing. Showing them drafts of writing is a very eye-opening experience for them. Showing them drafts of a published poem can open up a whole world. The Children's Literature Research Collections held at the Kerlan Collection of the University of Minnesota offer a unique resource for sharing poetry with children: a portfolio of materials donated by Barbara Esbensen. The Barbara Esbensen Poetry Portfolio is multimedia learning tool that uses her work to highlight her versatility as a writer, poet, and storyteller. The kit is appropriate for grades 2 through 8 and includes lessons, biographical information, supporting documents, and overhead transparencies of manuscript pages and galleys of Esbensen's writing. This can be invaluable for helping children understand the process of writing and publishing poetry. Aspiring writers, in particular, will find this "behind-the-scenes" view fascinating. They may even be brave enough to share their own first drafts and final copies! For more information, go to: http://special.lib.umn.edu/clrc/esbensen/. In addition, Esbensen offers a resource for adults, who want additional insight in teaching poetry effectively, entitled *A Celebration Of Bees: Helping Children Write Poetry* (Holt, 1995).

Aileen Fisher

AILEEN FISHER'S BIO

Aileen Fisher was born in Iron River, Michigan, on September 9, 1906, and died in 2002 at age 96. She attended the University of Chicago from 1923 to 1925 and received her bachelor's degree in journalism in 1927 from the University of Missouri. She lived in Boulder, Colorado, all of her adult life and her interests included woodworking, hiking, and mountain climbing. During her career she worked as director of the Women's National Journalistic Register in Chicago from 1928 to 1931; a research assistant for the Labor Bureau of the Middle West in Chicago from 1931 to 1932, and then as a freelance writer beginning in 1932. She published her first book of poetry for children, *The Coffee Pot Face* (Robert M. McBride & Co.) in 1933.

She was an award-winning author of over 100 children's books, including poetry, plays, short stories, picture books, and biographies. Aileen Fisher was the second winner of the NCTE Award for Excellence in Poetry for Children in 1978.

AILEEN FISHER'S POETRY

For a compilation of some of Aileen Fisher's most popular poems, look for *I Heard a Bluebird Sing* (Boyds Mills Press, 2002). This volume features 41 Fisher poems chosen by children, along with excerpts of interviews with and articles by Fisher about her life and her work. Her simplicity and directness shine through these poems, often reflecting a childlike point of view about the natural world. Also look for her collection, *Always Wondering: Some Favorite Poems of Aileen Fisher* (HarperCollins, 1991) to read the poet's own favorite poems including some of the most requested poems from her own work. In both cases, these anthologies represent a selection based on reader input. Invite the children to conduct their own survey or poll of favorite poems—of Fisher's or others. Gather the votes and post the favorites list. Consider having children read and record these favorites much like poet Robert Pinsky's Favorite Poem Project, which has average citizens audiotaping their favorite poems (http://www.favoritepoem.org/). In addition, they may also enjoy the nature poems of Lilian Moore, Constance Levy, Kristine O'Connell George, and Michio Mado.

Many, many of Fisher's poetry collections are focused specifically on animals and animal life. For example, *Rabbits, Rabbits* (Harper, 1983) captures the life of a rabbit in 21 poems and *The House of a Mouse* (Harper, 1988) is a collection of poems about mice describing where they live, what they eat, and how they look. The poems are crystallized descriptions written with strong rhythms. Plus they are simple and engaging enough for even the youngest listener to enjoy. Connect these works with other collections of animal poems, such as *Animals, Animals* illustrated by Eric Carle (Scholastic, 1989) or *The Beauty of the Beast* compiled by Jack Prelutsky (Knopf, 1997). Read the poems out loud with animal puppets to mouth the words.

Aileen Fisher has also authored many picture storybooks about animals and nature told in rhyme that are on our library shelves. Many have even been reissued in recent years, including: *You Don't Look Like Your Mother* (Mondo, 2001), *Know What I Saw* (Roaring Brook Press, 2005), and *The Story Goes On* (Roaring Brook Press, 2005). These are also excellent examples of her sensitive and playful treatment of nature themes all told in rhyme. Complement these with simple nonfiction books that provide factual information about the natural world such as Jean Craighead George's *One Day* series, for example *One Day in the Woods* (HarperTrophy, 1988) or Ken Robbins' *The Elements* series, such as *Earth: The Elements* (Holt, 1995).

Fisher has also authored poems that focus on the earth and sky: *Sing of the Earth and Sky: Poems about Our Planet and the Wonders Beyond* (Boyds Mills Press, 2003). Here, she turns her gift for observation to the subjects of the earth, sun, moon, and stars with thoughtful poems that inspire reflection. Look for other similar poetry anthologies like Barbara Brenner's *The Earth is Painted Green: A Garden of Poems about Our Planet* (Scholastic, 1994) or *The Sun in Me: Poems About the Planet* compiled by Judith Nicholls (Barefoot Books, 2003) or Jane Yolen's *Color Me a Rhyme: Nature Poems for Young People* (Wordsong/Boyds Mills Press, 2000). Bring these together to share during Earth Day celebrations or for earth science units of instruction. Children can choose favorite poems to copy onto "globe" shapes to display.

Paul Fleischman

http://www.paulfleischman.net/

PAUL FLEISCHMAN'S BIO

Paul Fleischman was born on September 5 in Monterey, California, and grew up in Santa Monica, California, son of Newbery award winning author, Sid Fleischman. He grew up enjoying bicycle explorations with his sisters, playing the piano, making sculptures out of driftwood and found objects, and tinkering with the family's printing press. Fleischman studied at the University of California at Berkeley, but completed his bachelor's degree several years later at the University of New Mexico. In between he traveled across the United States by bicycle and train and lived for a time in New Hampshire in a 200-year-old house in the woods. Eventually he turned to writing beginning with historical novels for young people and has since published many award-winning books in nearly every genre, including poetry.

PAUL FLEISCHMAN'S POETRY

Paul Fleischman has earned a reputation as one of the most innovative, gifted, and versatile authors in the field of children's literature. His complex, unconventional narratives are regarded as challenging for young readers but also rewarding because of their emotional depth. Fleischman has received overwhelming critical praise for the grace and lyricism of his prose and poetry. Critics also note vivid imagery and authentic characters among the many strengths of his works. Fleischman has won numerous awards, including a Newbery Honor Book citation for *Graven Images* (HarperCollins, 1982); the Newbery Medal for *Joyful Noise* (HarperCollins, 1988); and the Scott O'Dell Award for *Bull Run* (HarperCollins, 1993), among many others. In fact, *Joyful Noise* was even recognized as one of the "100 Best Books of the Century" by *School Library Journal* in 2000.

The author's emphasis on the sound of language may be most prominent in his poetry collections: *I Am Phoenix: Poems for Two Voices* (HarperCollins, 1985), poems about the warbler, cormorant, passenger pigeon, egret, sparrow, owl, and other birds and *Joyful Noise: Poems for Two Voices* (HarperCollins, 1988), which includes the voices of crickets, honey bees, cicadas, and other insects. These challenging poems for two voices are excellent for children in the middle grades. They require synchronization of reading as well as getting used to two completely different lines sometimes being read at the same time. Paul Fleischman's poems may indeed be the best-known examples of poems written for two voices. With practice, students can master the two-voice arrangement, and then they may be ready to tackle poems for four voices, Fleischman's *Big Talk: Poems for Four Voices* (Candlewick, 2000), with subjects ranging from ghosts to gossip to grandma. Partner this book with Eloise Greenfield's book, *The Friendly Four* (HarperCollins, 2006), which also features roles for four readers.

For audio adaptations, both *I am Phoenix* and *Joyful Noise* are available from HarperAudio, so listeners can hear how the poems should sound when read by asynchronous and overlapping voices. It is also possible to access some audiofiles of poetry read aloud and available on the Internet. For example, Audible.com, a major provider of audiobooks via downloadable files offers Paul Fleischman's *Joyful Noise* online. Children may even enjoy recording their own oral readings on tapes or CDs. The truly ambitious might like to create a slide show presentation with images of each bird or insect accompanied by a student-created audio track of the corresponding poems.

And of course Fleischman's bird and insect poems in *I am Phoenix* and *Joyful Noise* lend themselves beautifully to science study. For example, these poems can be paired with Laurence Pringle's nonfiction picture books *An Extraordinary Life: The Story of a Monarch Butterfly* (Orchard, 1997) or *A Dragon in the Sky: The Story of a Green Darner Dragonfly* (Scholastic, 2001). Children may want to conduct their own observations of local birds or insects. For a poetic example of a science notebook look for Kristine O'Connell George's *Hummingbird Nest: A Journal of Poems* (Harcourt, 2004). Nature is the dominant theme in her poetry collections. Supplement these with Marilyn Singer's poem collections, *Turtle in July* (Macmillan, 1989) and *Fireflies at Midnight* (Atheneum, 2003), in which she mimics the rhythms and sounds of the animals she portrays. Or after reading aloud *Creepy Crawlies* (Ainsworth, 2000), children can refer to the book to construct models of insects with marshmallows and toothpicks.

Contrast Fleischman's poetry with another poet who has written poems expressly for two voices, Georgia Heard. Her poem "Fishes," for example, is one of many in this format in *Creatures of Earth, Sea, and Sky* (Wordsong/Boyds Mills Press, 1992). Other poems, not necessarily written for two voices, can also be adapted for performance with two voices by the arrangement or rearrangement of the lines. Some lines can be identified for Voice 1 or Voice 2, with key lines designated for both voices. It takes practice, but poems for two voices are almost magical when read aloud. One can even find poems that may not be intended for two voices reading, but may be very effective delivered that way. For example, Jennifer Clement's poem, Arbol de Limon/ Lemon Tree" appears in both Spanish and English (translated by Consuelo de Aerenlund) in Naomi Shihab Nye's collection, *This Tree is Older Than You Are* (Simon & Schuster, 1995). If there is a Spanish speaker volunteer in the audience, she/he can read the poem in Spanish, followed by a reading in English. Then *both* readers read their version simultaneously, in both Spanish and English. Just be sure to encourage the readers to pause at the end of each line and start the next line together. The effect is quite stunning.

Ralph Fletcher

http://www.ralphfletcher.com/

RALPH FLETCHER'S BIO

Ralph Fletcher was born on March 17, the oldest of nine children. He earned his bachelor's degree from Dartmouth College and his Master of Fine Arts degree from Columbia University in New York. He is married to JoAnn Portalupi and they have four sons. He has written poetry, picture books, chapter books for older readers, transitional readers, and professional books for educators. Fletcher has worked as an educational consultant and writer working with teachers and children across the United States, in Europe, and in the Middle East.

RALPH FLETCHER'S POETRY

Ralph Fletcher has created one collection of poetry that expresses the sadness many children feel when they have to move to a new place, *Moving Day* (Wordsong/Boyds Mills, 2006). The poems are loosely connected one to another to reveal the grieving process of separating from the familiar and slowly establishing new roots in a new place. Although each poem can stand alone, each has even greater impact when read as a story narrative. The poems are grounded in familiar moments and images (a new bike, an old sweatshirt) that become metaphors for deeper feelings. This collection is a reassuring voice for children who are dealing with one of life's most challenging transitions. A similar collection, *Relatively Speaking: Poems about Family* (Orchard, 1999) depicts more ordinary family events also from the point of view of a younger brother told through connected free verse poems. Look for similar poem-stories for boys by Gary Soto: *Fearless Fernie: Hanging Out with Fernie & Me* (Putnam, 2002) and *Worlds Apart: Fernie and Me* (Putnam, 2005). Encourage boys to share their responses to these poems. Look for http://www.guysread.com for additional tips on engaging boy readers, in particular.

If you're looking for "love" poems for Valentine's Day, you won't have much trouble. Poets have been pouring out their hearts for centuries. "How do I love thee, let me count the ways," wrote Elizabeth Barrett Browning to her sweetheart, Robert Browning. Young readers feel this same longing and often gravitate to very emotional "love" poetry—both in their reading and in their writing. You might even be surprised how popular these can be with adolescent readers (both boys and girls). Ralph Fletcher has created an entire book of love poetry for young readers called *I Am Wings; Poems About Love*

(Atheneum, 1994), dividing this small collection into two sections: "Falling in (love)" and "Falling out (of love)." One of the most notable poems is "Owl Pellets" which compares dissection in biology to the pain of rejection. For the girl's point of view, consider Angela Shelf Medearis' poem, "Boys" from her collection, *Skin Deep and Other Teenage Reflections* (Macmillan, 1995). Fletcher has another collection of love poems entitled *Buried Alive* which was republished along with *I Am Wings* in a compilation entitled *Room Enough for Love* (Aladdin, 1998).

Ralph Fletcher has also authored poetry collections with nature themes including *Water Planet: Poems about Water* (Arrowhead, 1991), *Ordinary Things: Poems from a Walk in Early Spring* (Atheneum, 1996), and *Have You Been to the Beach Lately?* (Orchard, 2001). These poems urge one to go outside and experience nature firsthand, take notes or photographs, and describe a favorite outdoor spot. Connect these works with *Splash! Poems Of Our Watery World* (Orchard, 2002) by Constance Levy or *How to Cross a Pond: Poems About Water* (Knopf, 2003) by Marilyn Singer, both collections of free verse poems about water in all its forms. Follow up with the highly acclaimed nonfiction book, *A Drop of Water: A Book of Science and Wonder* (Scholastic, 1997) by Walter Wick. Gather magazine pictures or Web photographs of a variety of forms of water and post them with accompanying poems.

Fletcher has also created many books *about* poetry writing, including one especially for children who want to write: *A Writing Kind of Day: Poems for Young Poets* (Boyds Mills Press, 2005). This poetry book offers "advice" poems for young people who want to express themselves through poetry writing. Pair this with his nonfiction work for young writers, *Poetry Matters: Writing a Poem from the Inside Out* (Atheneum, 1997). Children can find additional inspiration and assistance with their poetry writing from Web sites such as "Poetry Hill Poetry" at http://www.potatohill.com. This site is rich with ideas for sharing poems and poetry writing with children of all ages, including poetry writing contests for kids, poems written by children of all ages, and teacher resources and workshop information.

And for adults who work with children, particularly educators, Fletcher has created a small library of resource books that are very clear and helpful including *A Writer's Notebook* (HarperTrophy, 2003), *Craft Lessons* (Stenhouse, 1998), and *Boy Writers; Reclaiming Their Voices* (Stenhouse, 2006), among others. His personal Web site provides additional guidance with lesson plans for educators and tips for child writers.

Douglas Florian

DOUGLAS FLORIAN'S POETRY

Douglas Florian's poetry is known for its humor, wordplay, and clever description, accompanied by unique artistic creations on paper bags, with paint, ink or rubber stamps, etc. In addition, many of his picture book collections are organized thematically around various animal groups including:

Beast Feast (Harcourt, 1994)

On the Wing (Harcourt, 1996)

In the Swim (Harcourt, 1997)

Insectlopedia (Harcourt, 1998

Mammalabilia (Harcourt, 2000)

Lizards, Frogs, and Polliwogs (Harcourt, 2001)

Bow Wow Meow Meow (Harcourt, 2003)

Omnibeasts (Harcourt, 2004)

Zoo's Who (Harcourt, 2005)

These form a small library of their own featuring both visual and verbal creations of all kinds of animals. Many of the poems provide both a great deal of factual information, as well as fun wordplay and internal rhyme. Challenge children to gather parallel nonfiction books about animals to look up the facts they glean from Florian's animal poetry. Encourage them to use new facts in poems of their own creation. They may also enjoy the animal poetry found in *Leap into Poetry* (Wordsong/Boyds Mills Press, 2001) by Avis Harley or *A Hippopotamustn't: And Other Animal Poems* (Dial, 1990) by J. Patrick Lewis.

In addition, Florian has created four completely different kinds of poetry books that focus on the seasons of the year including *Handsprings* (Greenwillow, 2006), *Summersaults* (Greenwillow, 2002), *Autumnblings* (Greenwillow, 2003), and *Winter Eyes* (Greenwillow, 1999). These also contain descriptive poetry vignettes, but each is illustrated with lovely, playful scenic watercolors. Contrast Florian's seasonal collection with Francisco X. Alarcón's four bilingual picture books of poetry for the four seasons. Follow up with simple nonfiction picture books, such as Seymour Simon's books: *Autumn across America* (Hyperion, 1993), *Winter across America* (Hyperion, 1994), and *Spring across America* (Hyperion, 1996), all illustrated with vivid photographs of the seasons.

If you have to choose just one title by Florian, however, *Bing Bang Boing* (Harcourt, 1994) might be the best choice, with its companion volume, *Laugheteria* (Harcourt, 1999) close behind. Although they don't have the lush, colorful illustrations of his shorter picture book anthologies, they are jam-packed full of rhythmic, humorous poetry that appeals to nearly all age levels. The odd and interesting pen and ink sketches and the zany sensibility are very reminiscent of Shel Silverstein's poetry. And so many of these Florian poems lend themselves to choral reading, too. Here are just a few examples. One poem that has been irresistible to first graders through fourth graders is "My Monster" by Douglas Florian (*Bing Bang Boing*). Although, teachers must have a sense of humor about the endlines: "That's no monster, that's my teacher!" Once students are familiar with poems read aloud, two groups can read poems aloud in a "call and response" method. The best poems for this poetry performance strategy are those whose lines are structured in a kind of back and forth way. One example for two groups to read aloud in this back-and-forth manner is "Twins" by Douglas Florian from *Bing Bang Boing*.

Some poems are list-like in their structure and these work well for what is sometimes called "linearound" choral reading in which individual voices read individual lines. Florian's "Delicious Wishes" is ideal for solo line reading (*Bing Bang Boing*) with each child taking a different wish (e.g., "I wish I could whistle") to read and act out. Many poems lend themselves to incorporating movement by acting out verbs or highlighting vocabulary. Douglas Florian's "The Bully" from *Bing Bang Boing* provides numerous action phrases, for example.

Finally, one last strategy for performing poetry is singing poems. While not a particularly complex method, it is irresistibly fun. Students of all ages and language backgrounds love the connection of music and poetry. Basically, you match poems to song tunes that contain the same meter. It seems to be most effective with tunes that have a strong, rhythmic beat such as "Row, Row, Row Your Boat" or "Mary Had A Little Lamb" and poems that are very rhythmic. One all-time favorite has been "School Cafeteria" by Douglas Florian (*Bing Bang Boing*), a hilarious poem about cafeteria food that can be sung to the tune "Ninety-Nine Bottles Of Pop" and begins "Nothing is drearier than my school cafeteria."

Another option for creative poem sharing is to link art and poetry. For Florian's poem, "What the Wind Swept Away Today" (*Bing Bang Boing*), children can create a picture for one line of the poem [e.g., "a purple leaf (off a tree)," "Someone's homework (graded D)"] to help them visualize the poem's list of objects that the wind blew away. After reading the poem and sharing the illustrations, they can also discuss the humor in the improbable event noted in the last line of the poem, "And my little sister Claire." Children can make monster masks out of paper plates to use as they acted out monster motions to accompany the oral reading of "A Monster's Day" (*Bing Bang Boing*). Children may also want to expand their artistic responses to imitate Florian's own art style through painting and collage. An excellent resource for even more creative poetry sharing ideas is Caroline Feller Bauer's *The Poetry Break: An Annotated Anthology with Ideas for Introducing Children to Poetry* (H. W. Wilson, 1995).

Helen Frost

http://www.helenfrost.net

HELEN FROST'S BIO

Helen Frost was born in Brookings, South Dakota, on September 3, 1949, one of ten children. She earned her bachelor's degree at Syracuse University in New York and her master's degree from Indiana University. She is married and is the mother of two sons. She has worked as a teacher in Scotland, Alaska, and Indiana and has long been involved in the YWCA and teen youth groups. She lives in Fort Wayne, Indiana, and her hobbies include hiking, cross-country skiing, kayaking, and raising and releasing monarch butterflies. Frost earned a prestigious Michael Printz honor distinction from the American Library Association for her first book of poetry for young people, *Keesha's House*. She has authored a play and a screenplay, as well as a resource book for adults who work with teen writers, *When I Whistle, Nobody Listens: Helping Young People Write about Difficult Issues* (Heinemann, 2001). Frost is also a prolific author of nonfiction series readers for young readers reflecting her interest in science and biology.

HELEN FROST'S POETRY

Helen Frost has written three novels-in-verse that are outstanding examples of how poems can be woven together to create a compelling narrative. Her first example, *Keesha's House* (Farrar, Straus & Giroux, 2003), was awarded a Michael Printz honor citation for young adult literature. This story is a series of monologues that weave together the perspectives of seven teenagers who each find their way to a "safe" house during troubled times in their lives. The format of multiple voices lends itself to dramatic read aloud. Seven volunteers can each take a different character and read his/her portions out loud seated "readers theater" style. There are plans in the works to adapt and film this book into a full-length feature film. Teens may enjoy discussing which actors they envision in each of the major roles. The Internet Movie Database (http://www.imdb.com) will offer updated information on filming, actors, director, etc.

Helen Frost's second novel-in-verse, *Spinning through the Universe: A Novel in Poems from Room 214* (Farrar, Straus & Giroux, 2004), focuses on a younger audience of fifth graders, their teacher, and the intersection of their lives in the classroom. Again, the book's format lends itself to multiple readers choosing parts and reading from the book as if it were a script.

Children can choose a favorite character from "Room 214" and draw a portrait of what they think she/he looks like. They can choose a representative poem in that character's voice and post it alongside their original drawing. To follow up, seek out other poetry books about classroom life, such as *Gracie Graves and the Kids from Room 402* (Harcourt Brace, 1995) by Betty Paraskevas or *Swimming Upstream: Middle School Poems* (Clarion, 2002) by Kristine O'Connell George. Fiction about school such as *Sideways Stories from Wayside School* (HarperTrophy, 2004) by Louis Sachar or the novel, *Sahara Special* (Hyperion, 2004) by Esme Raji Codell offer another perspective on classrooms, teachers, and school life.

In *The Braid* (Farrar, Straus & Giroux, 2006), Frost "braids" the intertwining tale of two sisters surviving hardships as Scottish refugees/immigrants in the 1850s. Told through a poetic structure of her own invention derived from Celtic knots (and explained in helpful endnotes), the story unfolds in narrative poems in two voices alternating with brief praise poems and all connected through parallel beginning and ending lines. Again, for reading aloud two girls could each take the role of a sister with the remaining volunteers reading the praise poems in between. Follow up by researching and experimenting with Celtic knots and braids. Choose a favorite praise poem and display it framed by a handmade braid or knot. Challenge readers to locate the geographical sites from the book (Scotland, Canada) on a map and trace the journey taken by each sister. Pair this book with a similar story of hardship and immigration set in Ireland during this same time period: *Nory Ryan's Song* (Delacorte, 2000) by Patricia Reilly Giff.

One of the most outstanding features of Foster's work is her creative use of poetic form in each of her books. This includes haiku, blank verse, sonnets, sestinas, rondelets, acrostics, and more. And she includes explanatory notes on these forms and her reasoning for choosing them for each book. Aspiring writers and poets may enjoy exploring this aspect of her writing in particular. If so, additional guidance and worksheets for trying different poetic formats are available on Foster's personal Web site. Children who want to read more works like Frost's may enjoy exploring the poetry of Craig Crist-Evans, Karen Hesse, and for older readers, Marilyn Nelson.

Kristine O'Connell George

http://www.kristinegeorge.com

KRISTINE O'CONNELL GEORGE'S BIO

Born on May 6, 1954 in Denver, Colorado, Kristine O'Connell George now lives in Southern California and grew up moving often from Ohio to Texas to Oregon in a family with three brothers. She now has one daughter of her own and is surrounded by all kinds of wildlife in her home in the mountains. Nature and animals are often the subjects of her writing. Her hobbies include sports like tennis, golf, and hiking as well as arts and crafts and photography.

Kristine O'Connell George burst onto the poetry scene winning the Lee Bennett Hopkins award in 1997 for her book, *The Great Frog Race and Other Poems*. This award is presented annually to an American poet or anthologist for the most outstanding new book of children's poetry published in the previous calendar year. In addition, she won the Lee Bennett Hopkins Promising Poet Award the following year in 1998. Her book, *Little Dog and Duncan* (Clarion, 2002) was the Claudia Lewis Award recipient in 2002 and *Hummingbird Nest: A Journal of Poems* (Harcourt, 2004) won the same award in 2004. The Claudia Lewis award is given annually to the best poetry book of the year by Bank Street College in New York.

KRISTINE O'CONNELL GEORGE'S POETRY

Kristine O'Connell George's poetry books include highly visual picture book collections on a variety of subjects. She has focused largely on nature themes and animal poems, but has also tackled middle-school experiences that many children can relate to. Children who enjoy poems about nature, animals, and experiences outdoors will particularly enjoy George's collections, *The Great Frog Race and Other Poems* (Clarion, 1997), *Old Elm Speaks: Tree Poems* (Clarion, 1998), and *Toasting Marshmallows: Camping Poems* (Clarion, 2001). These poems explore the natural world in fresh and playful imagery and language. Find a shady spot outside to read these poems or bring the outdoors in by pitching a small tent for quiet indoor reading of nature poems. Follow up with the nature poetry of Aileen Fisher, Constance Levy, and David McCord.

Little Dog Poems (Clarion, 1999) and it's sequel, *Little Dog and Duncan* (Clarion, 2002) are the perfect jumping off point for gathering other poetry books about dogs and puppies, such as *Bow Wow Meow Meow; It's Rhyming Cats and Dogs* by Douglas Florian (Harcourt, 2003), or *Dog Days: Rhymes Around the Year* collected by Jack Prelutsky (Knopf, 1999), or *It's About*

Dogs by Tony Johnston (Harcourt, 2000). These are the perfect addition to an evening showing of a dog movie or the annual pet adopt-a-thon day held in many communities.

George's book *Swimming Upstream: Middle School Poems* (Clarion, 2002) contains many poems that speak vividly to the experiences of older children. And the poem, "School Librarian" is a sympathetic portrait of a caring, empathetic school librarian. Share it to celebrate National Library Week or to use as an open invitation to the library any time. In this quiet, sensitive poem, George paints a picture of a particularly caring librarian who knows just which books to recommend to each reader. Read it aloud softly with a long pause between stanzas. Even better, have a student volunteer read it out loud. This may prompt a discussion of favorite "sad stories" complete with tissue bookmarks. Or as a follow up activity, make bookmarks listing favorite "sad stories" or gather a collection of unusual bookmarks you can find. Link this volume with the many poetry books for "tweens" and young teens by Sara Holbrook.

Hummingbird Nest: A Journal of Poems (Harcourt, 2004), beautifully illustrated by Barry Moser offers a series of poems full of observations of the emergence of hummingbirds from eggs in a nest. It is also an excellent companion to nonfiction life cycle books such as *An Extraordinary Life: The Story of a Monarch Butterfly* by Laurence Pringle (Orchard, 1997) or Lois Ehlert's book, *Waiting for Wings* (Harcourt, 2001). Young bird-watchers or butterfly watchers may want to keep their own journals about the local specimens they sight. Invite a local naturalist or expert to present further information.

George's collection, *Fold Me a Poem* (Harcourt, 2005), links each poem with an origami creation based on the Japanese art of paper folding. It is ideal for pairing origami activities with poem writing, particularly experimenting with Japanese poem forms such as haiku and tanka. Gather origami supplies (paper squares) and help children learn this unique craft of paper folding. Post their creations with the corresponding poems from the book or with new selections of their own choosing or writing.

Kristine O'Connell George's own Web site was chosen as an American Library Association "best web site" for families and kids. It is a rich resource for readers as well as aspiring poetry writers. Links include biographical information, a booklist, tips for teachers, varied activities for children, information about arranging an appearance, favorite quotes about poetry, and a guest book. In addition, she reads aloud over a dozen of her poems, in her "Poetry Aloud" link at http://www.kristinegeorge.com accessible via simple free software such as RealAudio or Windows Media.

Nikki Giovanni

http://www.nikki-giovanni.com

NIKKI GIOVANNI'S BIO

Nikki Giovanni was born Yolande Cornelia Giovanni, Jr., on June 7, 1943, in Knoxville, Tennessee. She earned her bachelor's degree from Fisk University, and completed postgraduate studies at University of Pennsylvania School of Social Work and Columbia University School of Fine Arts. She has received several honorary doctorates including one from Fisk University. She has taught at many colleges and universities and has been a professor at Virginia Polytechnic Institute in Blacksburg, Virginia, since 1987. She has given numerous poetry readings and lectures worldwide and appeared on many television and award programs. Her many awards include a Best Books for Young Adults citation from the American Library Association, the NAACP Image award, and the first Rosa Parks Woman of Courage Award.

NIKKI GIOVANNI'S POETRY

Although Nikki Giovanni may be best known for her poetry for adults, she has authored several significant collections for children:

> *Ego-Tripping and Other Poems for Young People* (Lawrence Hill, 1973)
>
> *Knoxville, Tennessee* (Scholastic, 1994)
>
> *Spin a Soft Black Song* (Farrar, Straus & Giroux, 1987)
>
> *The Sun Is So Quiet* (Holt, 1996)
>
> *Vacation Time: Poems for Children* (Morrow, 1980)

Frequently anthologized, Giovanni's poetry expresses strong racial pride and respect for family. In addition, many of her poems (for adults and children) are available in audio form in *The Nikki Giovanni Poetry Collection* (Harper-Audio, 2002).

Spin a Soft Black Song covers a wealth of childhood interests, such as basketball games, close friends, moms, and the coming of spring. "Poem for Rodney" finds a young man contemplating what he wants to be when he grows up. "If" reflects a young man's daydreams about what it might have been like to participate in a historic event. Pair these classic poems with the contemporary work of Charles R. Smith, Jr. such as *Rimshots: Basketball Pix, Rolls, and Rhythms* (Dutton, 1999) or *I Am America* (Scholastic, 2003) or with the stylized poetry of Arnold Adoff in *All the Colors of the Race* (Lothrop, Lee & Shepard, 1982) or *Street Music: City Poems* (HarperCollins, 1995).

Giovanni's free verse poem *Knoxville, Tennessee* celebrates the pleasures of home and summer time with family. Many of the warm images presented came directly from the author's childhood memories. Pair this with Eloise Greenfield's family-centered poem collection *Honey, I Love and Other Love Poems* (HarperCollins, 1978) or Nikki Grimes' celebratory *Hopscotch Love: A Family Treasury of Love Poems* (Lothrop, Lee & Shepard, 1999). For fiction counterparts, share the picture books *Bigmama's* by Donald Crews (HarperTrophy, 1998) or *We Had a Picnic This Sunday Past* by Jacqueline Woodson (Hyperion, 1998). Plan a poetry picnic for sharing these and other family poems outside spread out on a tablecloth.

Additional collections of Giovanni's poems focus on ordinary times of childhood from playtime to vacation time. Her book *The Sun Is So Quiet* is a collection of 13 poems ranging in topics from bedtime to missing teeth. In contrast, *Vacation Time* explores the world with a child's sense of discovery. Contrast Giovanni's style in these books with Barbara Esbensen's or Eve Merriam's writing. Children can bring postcards or souvenirs from their travels to display with these poems of vacation adventures.

Nikki Giovanni has also authored picture books, including *Rosa* (Holt, 2005) illustrated by Bryan Collier, a moving narrative tribute to Rosa Parks, as an individual and as a force for change in America. Connect this powerful Caldecott honor story with the classic poem by Countee Cullen, "Incident" (in *I, Too, Sing America: Three Centuries of African American Poetry* selected by Catherine Clinton, Houghton Mifflin, 1998), a vivid picture of racism which begins with "Once riding in old Baltimore." Here sadly, an eight-year-old child experiences bigotry directed at him by another child. For more rich poems about important African American figures and experiences, including "The Mother of the Movement (for Rose Parks)" look for Carole Boston Weatherford's poetry book, *Remember The Bridge: Poems of a People* (Philomel, 2002), beautifully illustrated with historic photographs and art.

Finally, for a reminder about the importance of the library, share Giovanni's poem, "ten years old" found in *Spin a Soft Black Son* as well as in many anthologies. It is told from the perspective of a 10-year-old African American child making a scary solo trip to the library. After reading the poem aloud, use four voices or parts to read the poem in parts: one for the first person narrator, one for the boy's dialogue, one for the librarian lines, and one for the line spoken by "another lady." Mark the lines of each reader with a highlighter to help them see their lines clearly. Find a copy of one of the *Doctor Dolittle* books by Hugh Lofting that is referred to in the poem and share it with the children. (They may be more familiar with film adaptations.) If possible, locate a stereoscope or viewfinder to demonstrate this device mentioned in the poem. Consider working together to create a National Poetry Month Time Capsule to capture today's poems for the future. Students can submit favorite poems or their own original writing. Put them in the Time Capsule and have a ceremonial sealing, not to be opened until National Poetry Month the next April.

Joan Bransfield Graham

http://www.joangraham.com/

JOAN BRANSFIELD GRAHAM'S BIO

Joan Bransfield Graham was born on Halloween, October 31, in Wildwood-by-the-sea, New Jersey. She grew up in that area and attended Rowan College in New Jersey, then the University of Wisconsin, UCLA and the University of San Francisco. She has been a teacher, scout leader, and outdoor education crafts instructor. Her hobbies include art, crafts, photography, traveling, camping, sailing, poetry, and reading. She lives near the Pacific Ocean in California with her husband, who is a former FBI agent.

JOAN BRANSFIELD GRAHAM'S POETRY

Joan Bransfield Graham's poetry books are wonderful examples of shape or concrete poetry in which the words of the poems are laid out on the page to suggest the subject of the poem. In both *Splish Splash* (Houghton Mifflin, 2001) and *Flicker Flash* (Houghton Mifflin, 2003), the graphic illustrations combine with the verbal descriptions of water or light in their many, varied forms.

Splish Splash celebrates the many forms that water can take, from ice cubes and icicles to waves and waterfalls, illustrated with vivid graphic designs by Steve Scott that are the perfect complement to each poem. The strong rhyme and word play provide a rare example of concrete poetry that works well on the page as well as for reading out loud. In fact, the strong use of onomatopoeia invites listeners to enjoy the sounds of the words. For example, when sharing the poem "Ice Cubes," bring a clear glass full of ice to "clink" and "click" and "clatter" when reading the poem. Create construction paper popsicles on wooden popsicle sticks to act out the "Popsicle" poem and avoid the "sticksicle," "dripsicle," "plopsicle" mess! For more water poems, look for Constance Levy's *Splash! Poems of Our Watery World* (Orchard, 2002), Marilyn Singer's *How to Cross a Pond: Poems about Water* (Knopf, 2003) and for informational book companions with photographic illustrations, seek out Walter Wick's *A Drop of Water* (Scholastic, 1997) or Ken Robbins' *Water: The Elements* (Holt, 1994).

The rhyming shape poems of *Flicker Flash* explore the different ways that *light* appears in our world, from the flicker of birthday candles to a flash of lightning. The ingenious illustrations by Nancy Davis feature bold graphic images that play with shape and type in creative ways and add to the impact of each poem. These are perfect selections to incorporate into science or art lessons. Read them aloud by a flashlight for added effect. In particular, read "Lamp" seated with the book near lamplight to demonstrate the poem's "lamp-shine." A natural complement is Anna Grossnickle Hines poetry book, *Winter Lights* (Greenwillow, 2005) or Marilyn Singer's *Central Heating: Poems about Fire and Warmth* (Knopf, 2005). Her poem "Lights Out" is ideal for sharing with Graham's "Lamp" poem—both about reading by the light of a lamp or flashlight. One note: several of Graham's poems in *Flicker Flash* deal with fire, including candles, matches, campfires, and fireworks. Each is beautifully described and illustrated and can lead to a helpful discussion of both metaphors as well as fire safety! Be very clear about proper procedures for handling fire-related objects like matches and candles, of course.

Children typically enjoy concrete poetry and take pleasure in the poet's creative use of the physical shape of the poem to convey meaning. It's a poetic form they like imitating and experimenting with. Concrete poetry also begs for artistic connection since the poems take the actual shape of their subject. Children can take other poems (or write their own) and copy them onto the shape of the subject, illustrating it any way they choose. They can create computer images or simple cut-and-paste collages similar to the illustrations in Graham's poetry books. They may enjoy creating a greeting card for someone special with a poem and drawing integrated together in a unique shape.

Follow up Graham's books with other examples of concrete poetry. J. Patrick Lewis's book, *Doodle Dandies: Poems that Take Shape* (Atheneum, 1998), *A Poke in the I: A Collection of Concrete Poems* (Candlewick, 2001) by Paul Janeczko, and Heidi Roemer's *Come to My Party* (Holt, 2004) are each delightful books of shape poetry, too. For a slightly more off-beat collection of concrete poems ideal for the pre-teen reader/writer check out *Technically, It's Not My Fault: Concrete Poems* (Clarion, 2004) by John Grandits.

Eloise Greenfield

ELOISE GREENFIELD'S POETRY

Eloise Greenfield is an acclaimed writer of prose and poetry for younger readers whose fiction is recognized for presenting strong portraits of loving African American families. Greenfield has authored books of poetry, picture books, biography, memoir, board books, and more, many of which have been illustrated by Jan Spivey Gilchrist. She teamed with her mother to create *Childtimes: A Three-Generation Memoir*, an autobiographical work that describes the childhood memories of Greenfield, her mother, and her maternal grandmother.

Greenfield's first collection of poetry for children, *Honey, I Love, and Other Love Poems* (HarperCollins, 1978), describes the experiences of a young black girl and deals with relationships involving family, friends, and schoolmates. This popular Reading Rainbow book is an amazing masterpiece from a poet who captures the unique dimensions of the African American experience (such as in her homage "Harriet Tubman"), while also tapping into the universal experiences of childhood (expressed in the wondering poem "By Myself"). From its small trim size to the Dillons' inviting black, white, and gold illustrations, these sixteen short poems capture feelings of love, grief, pride, and pleasure—all from the point of view of a child. It was republished as a stand-alone picture book with the same title by HarperCollins in 2003.

The poem, "Harriet Tubman" is strong and rhythmic narrative poem that invites children to join in on the repeated refrain which begins "Harriet Tubman didn't take no stuff." Pair Greenfield's poem with "The Conductor was a Woman" by Carole Boston Weatherford in *Remember The Bridge:*

Poems of a People (Philomel, 2002). This volume even includes a sepia-tone photograph of Tubman. Follow up with a picture book version of Harriet Tubman's life, *Minty: A Story of Young Harriet Tubman* (Dial, 1996) by Alan Schroeder, beautifully illustrated by Jerry Pinkney. Older children may also enjoy the nonfiction book, *Sojourner Truth: "Ain't I a Woman?* by Patricia McKissack and Fredrick McKissack (1992). Read aloud the chapter "Free Belle" or "Ain't I a Woman?" to lure readers in the middle grades to read the rest of her story on their own. Each of these chapters function as a story in itself about this fascinating woman and the times she lived in, first as a slave, then as a free woman.

Another standout poem from *Honey, I Love* offers a commentary on the value of poetry over "Things." In sharing this poem ("Things") aloud, invite the children to join in on the repeated line which occurs in the poem, "ain't got it no more." Participation is even easier if the stanza is held up on a large strip of paper or a display board. In Greenfield's book, *The Friendly Four* (HarperCollins, 2006), poems about the relationship of four special friends, the poem's lines are color-coded for participation and turn-taking. One poem, "At the Library" captures the enthusiasm of four readers looking for just the right book. Pair this with Nikki Grimes' poem of the same title from *It's Raining Laughter* (Dial, 1997). Greenfield has also gathered a whole collection of poems about books, words, and language entitled, *In the Land of Words* (HarperCollins, 2004). Share the poem "Books" or "I Don't Care" which capture the obsession with books and reading that so many avid readers feel. "Books" originally appeared on a Children's Book Week bookmark in 1979. Encourage children to choose their own favorite "book" poems and write them on a bookmark to savor again and again.

In her poetry, Greenfield tries to involve children in their own worlds. In *Night on Neighborhood Street* (Dial, 1991), Greenfield brings her young readers into the happenings around them examining the life of an urban community. The volume's seventeen poems show children in typical situations, including attending church and playing games with their families. Link this book with Carole Boston Weatherford's collection, *Sidewalk Chalk; Poems of the City* (Wordsong/Boyds Mills Press, 2001) with poems about the laundromat, local diner, city market, and barbershop, or Lilian Moore's *Mural on Second Avenue and Other City Poems* (Candlewick, 2005) which features poems about the city park, shop windows, skylines and bridges, and construction sites. Invite the children to list places they enjoy in their communities. What poems might they write to celebrate their favorite spots?

Eloise Greenfield created a memorable character in her poetry book, *Nathaniel Talking* (Writers & Readers Publishing, 1993) in which a nine-year-old boy shares his thoughts, dreams, and hopes in a series of first person poems. Match this collection with the *Danitra Brown* poetry books by Nikki Grimes for the girl's point of view. And look for Janet Wong's *Good Luck Gold and Other Poems* (Simon & Schuster, 1994) and *A Suitcase of Seaweed, and Other Poems* (Simon & Schuster, 1996) for more child perspectives on growing up in America.

For another view on culture, share Greenfield's *Under the Sunday Tree* (HarperCollins, 1988), a celebration of life in the Bahamas. Complement these poems with anthologies assembled by Caribbean poets John Agard and Grace Nichols, or consider *Under the Breadfruit Tree: Island Poems* (Boyds Mills Press, 1998) by Monica Gunning.

Nikki Grimes

http://www.nikkigrimes.com

NIKKI GRIMES' BIO

Nikki Grimes was born on October 20, 1950, in New York City. She began composing verse at the age of six, was published in high school, and has been writing ever since. She graduated in 1974 with a bachelor's degree from Rutgers University. In spite of a difficult childhood, her poetry often exudes optimism. She draws upon her own childhood experiences growing up as a young African American while addressing universal themes about family, friendship, and faith.

In addition to her work for children and young adults which numbers over 50 titles, Grimes has written articles for such magazines as *Essence, Today's Christian Woman, Book Links*, and *Image, the Journal of Arts & Religion*. During the 1970s, Nikki coproduced and hosted *The Kid's Show* on WBAI FM in New York. Later, during a six-year stint in Sweden, she hosted their radio program for immigrants and another for Swedish Educational Radio. Grimes has been a performing artist, fiber artist, jeweler, and photographer and currently lives in Corona, California.

Grimes is the 2006 recipient of the National Council of Teachers of English Excellence in Poetry Award. Grimes has won numerous other awards for her writing including: the Coretta Scott King Author Award, multiple Coretta Scott King Honor Book citations; Books for Youth Editors' Choice; American Library Association Notable Book, Cooperative Children's Book Center Best Choices, Bank Street College Best Books, New York Public Library 100 Books for Reading and Sharing, Chicago Library Best of the Best Books for Kids, NCTE Notable Children's Books in the Language Arts, *Horn Book* Fanfare, *Booklist* Editor's Choice, Junior Library Guild Selection, and many more.

NIKKI GRIMES' POETRY

Perhaps Nikki Grimes' most widely recognized poetic creation is the character of Danitra Brown. This spunky, young African American girl is a heroine to many readers and featured in poems in three different books:

* *Meet Danitra Brown* (Lothrop, Lee & Shepard, 1994)
* *Danitra Brown Leaves Town* (Lothrop, Lee & Shepard, 2002)
* *Danitra Brown, Class Clown* (Lothrop, Lee & Shepard, 2005)

After reading about her in these anthologies, children can try continuing her story by writing original poems of their own. What will Danitra do next? Create a large (life-size) cutout image of Danitra and post the new Danitra poems around her figure. Consider connecting Danitra with Eloise Greenfield's Nathaniel in *Nathaniel Talking* (Writers & Readers Publishing, 1993) or Lucille Clifton's character "Everett Anderson."

One of Grimes' most prominent topics in her poetry is the importance of family. Share poems from *Hopscotch Love: A Family Treasury of Love Poems* (Lothrop, Lee & Shepard, 1999), *My Man Blue* (Dial, 1999), and *Stepping Out with Grandma Mac* (Simon & Schuster, 2000). Invite children to share stories of experiences they have enjoyed with favorite family members. They might choose a favorite Grimes poem to take home and share with their own families. Link these family poems with family fiction, such as the novels of Christopher Paul Curtis or Angela Johnson.

Young writers who enjoy keeping a journal may enjoy poring over two of Grimes' works: *Jazmin's Notebook* (Dial, 1998) and *A Dime a Dozen* (Dial, 1998). Through first person poems, these two collections share a child's point of view on her life and her surroundings. Young writers may want to experiment with journaling in poetic form, as well as through writing narratives. They may also be surprised to find poetry used to build a biography as in Grimes' picture book, *Talkin' 'bout Bessie: The Story of Aviator Elizabeth Coleman* (Orchard, 2002). Here the subject (Bessie) is revealed through poems from the perspectives of many people who knew her or encountered her. Children might enjoy trying poetry for their autobiographical or biographical writing. Teen readers will respond to *Bronx Masquerade* (Dial, 2001), a novel with poems written as if they were penned by teenagers themselves in many strong and varied voices.

Grimes' own travels have shaped her poetry writing in these two collections: *Tai Chi Morning: Snapshots of China* (Cricket Books, 2004) and *Is It Far to Zanzibar? Poems about Tanzania* (HarperCollins, 2000). Locate each country on a world map and research additional information via atlases or the Internet. What facts and details can readers glean from the poems? What feelings and impressions does she convey about each country, too? Combine these poetry books with nonfiction books about China or Tanzania. What do we learn from each source?

For those interested in Nikki Grimes' poetry with a religious focus, look for these collections: *At Break of Day* (Eerdman's Books for Young Readers, 1999), *When Daddy Prays* (Eerdman's Books for Young Readers, 2002), *At Jerusalem's Gate* (Eerdman's Books for Young Readers, 2005), and *Come Sunday* (Eerdman's Books for Young Readers, 1996). These have a definite Christian perspective with a thoughtful or celebratory tone. Readers looking for poems for devotionals or to supplement lessons, will find these beautifully illustrated picture book collections enjoyable.

For a celebration of the library, look for Grimes' poem, "At the Library" in *It's Raining Laughter* (Boyds Mills Press, 2004). The poem depicts a "brownskin girl" who is "skinny, but she's strong, and brave, and wise" and finds adventure and escape in the pages of library books. This poem also lends itself to reading in two groups, by couplets. One group reads the first two lines, the other group reads the next two lines, continuing alternating back and forth. Afterward, children could work together to create a mural or sidewalk chalk art depicting the wonders found in books—for example, those mentioned in the poem: crystal seas, pirates hiding, talking birds, flying children, and walking trees, among others. Partner this poem with Patricia McKissack's picture book, *Goin' Someplace Special* (Atheneum, 2001) where a young African American girl finds the library is a welcome haven, one of the few integrated places in her 1950s southern community.

Monica Gunning

MONICA GUNNING'S POETRY

Monica Gunning's writing has focused on capturing her own experiences of life in the Caribbean with vivid description and imagery. She has also turned her attention to the experiences of the immigrant in the United States and has written both poetry and prose (*A Shelter In Our Car*, Children's Book Press, 2004) to tell some of those stories. As an immigrant herself, she understands the duality of having two "homes." Her work includes both celebration and longing in language that is fresh and musical.

Her first poetry collection, *Not a Copper Penny in Me House* (Wordsong/Boyds Mills Press, 1999) includes 15 poems that evoke the sights and sounds of the Caribbean. Subjects range from washing clothes to an outdoor classroom to Grand Market Street on Christmas Eve to a tropical hurricane. A sense of pride in home and family emerges through this series of unrhymed, lyrical poems. It begs comparison to other collections of Caribbean poetry for children including John Agard and Grace Nichols's anthology *A Caribbean Dozen* (Candlewick, 1994) or Lynn Joseph's *A Coconut Kind of Day* (Lothrop, 1990). Broaden their knowledge beyond the "Pirates of the Caribbean" movies, to consider the many different islands, cultures, and histories present in this area. In contrast, children can examine other collections of "neighborhood" poetry such as Carole Boston Weatherford's *Sidewalk Chalk; Poems of the City* (Wordsong/Boyds Mills Press, 2001) or Lilian Moore's *Mural on Second Avenue and Other City Poems* (Candlewick, 2005).

Gunning's second book of poetry, *Under the Breadfruit Tree: Island Poems* (Wordsong/Boyds Mills Press, 1998) includes 36 more poems, all strongly rooted in Caribbean people and culture. A similar assortment of characters and experiences come to life in this slightly more serious collection including an aunt who tells Anansi stories, a Grandma who trades cane from the fields, and the unexpected death of a friend. For children who are not already familiar with Anansi stories, this is a natural extension activity—sharing the classic Anansi picture book by Gerald McDermott or more Caribbean-flavored versions of Anancy stories by James Berry. On a more serious note, another possible book extension is sharing Regina Hanson's thoughtful picture book, *A Season for Mangoes* (Clarion, 2005). In this story set in Jamaica, Sareen is allowed to attend her first all-night "sit-in," a Jamaican tradition, to honor her grandmother who has recently died. Everyone in attendance is encouraged to share stories and memories of the deceased, while also enjoying traditional foods and participating in customary games and activities. Sareen finds the courage to tell about her Nana's love of mangoes and her love for life.

In her poetry collection, *America, My New Home* (Boyds Mills Press, 2004), Gunning writes about a contemporary immigrant child "far from my Jamaica sea foam" adjusting with difficulty to her new home. The simple poems and upbeat scenes contrast the busy urban landscape with the more intimate island life. The honest appraisal of what is missed (people know you by name) and what is gained (large libraries, magnificent symphonies) adds real poignancy. Partner this book with Jorge Argueda's *A Movie in My Pillow/Una película en mi almohada* (Children's Book Press, 2001) for another viewpoint. And for the library setting, share Gunning's powerful poem, "The Library" which observes: "In my village,/Grandpa's well-used Bible/was the only book I knew." Discuss with the children which books, toys, or memories they especially treasure.

Avis Harley

AVIS HARLEY'S BIO

Avis Harley grew up in British Columbia, Canada. She earned a master's degree and has spent most of her career in the field of education. She has taught elementary school in England, Canada, and at the University of British Columbia. While working in Canada she became involved with a program mentoring young poets. She is now retired from teaching and focuses on giving poetry workshops. Harley is married and has a son. She has many hobbies including drawing, gardening, singing, and opera.

AVIS HARLEY'S POETRY

Avis Harley's poetry writing is characterized by its diversity and experimentation. She enjoys trying poetry in all its different formats and is adept at demonstrating poetic form for children. Her first collection *Fly With Poetry: An ABC of Poetry* (Wordsong/Boyds Mills Press, 2000) includes 27 original short poems, generally one for each letter of the alphabet such as acrostics, blank verse, cinquain, etc. In addition, a brief definition of the form is provided as a caption at the bottom of each page. Fourteen additional poetic forms are shared in the back of the book. This is a tremendous resource for children who want to try their own hands at creating poetry. Harley's poem examples are brief, vivid, and clear. An excellent companion book is Paul Janeczko's *Poetry from A to Z: A Guide to Young Writers* (Simon & Schuster, 1994), also arranged alphabetically with additional poetic forms and examples by a variety of poets. Another poet who experiments extensively with poetic format is Helen Frost whose longer works for older readers incorporate haiku, blank verse, sonnets, sestinas, rondelets, and acrostics, along with explanatory endnotes.

Harley has a second volume of poetry organized around the same alphabet theme, *Leap into Poetry* (Wordsong/Boyds Mills Press, 2001). In this book, she provides 26 poems about insects, each demonstrating another poetic form or literary term, such as "jargon" or "karanamala." Once again, each term is also defined in a single line across the bottom of the page. In this case, children can further explore the topic of insects with Douglas Florian's poems *Insectlopedia* (Harcourt, 1998) or look for other poem writing resource books such as *A Kick in the Head: An Everyday Guide to Poetic Forms* by Paul Janeczko (Candlewick, 1994). For more examples of poetic experimentation, consult many of Myra Cohn Livingston's poetry collections, for example, *Cricket Never Does: A Collection of Haiku and Tanka*

(McElderry, 1997). Challenge the children to work as a group to create a new alphabet book of poems on the topic of their choice, with each child responsible for one letter of the alphabet with a corresponding poem or poetic form.

Avis Harley used color photographs as the centerpiece for her book *Sea Stars: Saltwater Poems* (Wordsong/Boyds Mills Press, 2006) illustrated by Margaret Butschler. Each of these 27 poems was inspired by a photograph of a sea creature, and again Harley incorporates a variety of poetic forms—including rhyming couplets, haiku, tanka, and nursery rhyme parody. The poems are brief, well-crafted and clever, full of wordplay, and accompanied by exquisite images. Brief endnotes provide additional information about each sea creature. Again, Douglas Florian's descriptive wordplay poems in *In the Swim* (Harcourt, 1997) provide an interesting parallel, and readers can contrast the use of photographs versus paintings for the illustrations of the sea creatures.

David L. Harrison

DAVID L. HARRISON'S BIO

David Harrison was born on March 13, 1937, in Springfield, Missouri, and earned his bachelor's degree in zoology from Drury College, his master's degree in parasitology from Emory University, and completed graduate studies at Evansville University. He is married with two children. He has worked as a pharmacologist, editorial manager, business owner, and as a professional musician, music teacher, and principal trombonist in the Springfield Symphony. Harrison has served on school boards and as a college trustee and is active in several literacy organizations. He has led several literacy service projects including raising 181,000 new books for school libraries

DAVID HARRISON'S POETRY

David Harrison has published more than 65 books of fiction, nonfiction, and poetry for young people, as well as a dozen books under the pseudonym "Kennon Graham" and "Arthur Kennon Graham." His first book of poetry, *Somebody Catch My Homework* (Boyds Mills Press, 1993) became an International Reading Association Children's Choice book and inspired a play adaptation. Two other poetry books were also honored on the Children's Choices list including *When Cows Come Home* (Boyds Mills Press, 1994) and *A Thousand Cousins* (Boyds Mills Press, 1996). His poem, "My Book," is sandblasted into the sidewalk at a library in Phoenix, Arizona. Harrison has also authored or collaborated on several resource books including two teaching strategy books, *Easy Poetry Lessons That Dazzle and Delight* (Scholastic, 1999), as well as a book for young writers, *Writing Stories: Fantastic Fiction from Start to Finish* (Sagebrush, 2004).

One of Harrison's best known collections of poetry is *Somebody Catch My Homework: Poems* (Boyds Mills Press, 1993), which features a variety of poems addressing the trials and tribulations children often have in school. Missing-homework excuses, asking timely permission for restroom privileges, and complaints about playground bullies are set to verse with a sense of humor that is accessible to children. Combine this collection with other hilarious poetry about school by writers such as Kalli Dakos (*If You're Not Here, Please Raise Your Hand*, Four Winds Press, 1990) or Carol Diggory Shields (*Almost Late to School and More School Poems*, Dutton, 2003).

In *When Cows Come Home* (Boyds Mills Press, 1994), Harrison reveals what really happens on the farm when the farmer's back is turned; "You never saw / Such cow horseplay / When Farmer looks / The other way!" Parallel these cow adventures with Doreen Cronin's picture book, *Click Clack Moo: Cows That Type* (Simon & Schuster, 2000) and Alice Schertle's cow poem collection, *How Now, Brown Cow?* (Voyager, 1998).

The topic of family is the focus of Harrison's poetry collection *A Thousand Cousins: Poems of Family Life* (Boyds Mills Press, 1996), a lighthearted look at typical family situations. The poet explores the relationships between siblings and extended family members and makes light of situations such as fathers snoring and mothers scolding. Similar situations often pop up in the poetry of Shel Silverstein, Jack Prelutsky, and Judith Viorst. These family poems lend themselves to hilarious role playing with dramatic read aloud. They particularly relish performing parent parts!

David Harrison has also created an autobiographical poetry collection, *Connecting Dots: Poems of My Journey* (Boyds Mills Press, 2004) with poetic snapshots of his past which he describes as "dots" to connect in order to create a picture of his life. It serves as a model for how children can create their own autobiographies through poetry, along with Lee Bennett Hopkins' autobiographical *Been to Yesterdays* (Wordsong/Boyds Mills Press, 1995) and Kathi Appelt's *My Father's Summers* (Holt, 2004).

Georgia Heard

GEORGIA HEARD'S BIO

Georgia Heard was born in Enterprise, Alabama on December 13, 1957. She attended American University, the University of New Hampshire and received a Master of Fine Arts degree in poetry writing from Columbia University. She is a landscape painter as well as a writer, and has shown paintings in several exhibitions. She serves on the Art in Public Places board in her home city and also enjoys kayaking and traveling throughout the world. She is married and has a son.

Heard is also a frequent speaker and advocate for poetry and poetry writing. She's been interviewed on National Public and worked for seven years with New York City teachers as part of the Teachers College Writing Project. She is also the author of several popular books on teaching poetry and writing to children including:

For the Good of the Earth and Sun: Teaching Poetry (Heinemann, 1987)

Writing Toward Home: Tales & Lessons to Find Your Way (Heinemann, 1995)

Awakening the Heart: Exploring Poetry in Elementary and Middle School (Heinemann, 1999)

The Revision Toolbox: Teaching Techniques That Work (Heinemann, 2002)

GEORGIA HEARD'S POETRY

Georgia Heard's first collection of poetry, *Creatures of Earth, Sea, and Sky* (Boyds Mills, 1997) focuses on the animal world and incorporates a variety of poetic forms, including poems for two voices ready to be performed out loud. Pair this with Paul Fleischman's collections for two voices, *I Am Phoenix* (HarperCollins, 1985) and *Joyful Noise* (HarperCollins, 1988), or with Douglas Florian's animal anthology, *Omnibeasts* (Harcourt, 2004). Nature magazines like *Ranger Rick* and *National Geographic* can supplement with photographs and current news.

Georgia Heard compiled the poem anthology, *Songs of Myself: An Anthology of Poems and Art* (Mondo, 2000) with works by many major children's poets. Along with Mary Ann Hoberman's anthology, *My Song is Beautiful: Poems and Pictures in Many Voices* (Little, Brown, 1994), both beautifully illustrated collections focus on identity and self concept and can help promote discussion. Children may want to create their own self-portraits or use photographs to prompt poem writing about their own goals, hopes, worries, and dreams.

A powerful collection, *This Place I Know: Poems of Comfort* (Candlewick, 2002/2006), was Heard's special project following the September 11 tragedy. It is a tender tribute, but offers an even broader perspective on pain, suffering, grief, and hope by many notable poets. Children may be moved to share their own stories of loss or draw pictures depicting their concerns.

In her professional books, Heard offers practical tips that are invaluable for promoting a poetry-friendly environment. She encourages children to create a "living anthology." In *Awakening the Heart*, she says, "Instead of collecting poems we love and putting them in a book, we'll make an anthology out of the walls and spaces around the school [or library]. It will be our jobs to make sure poetry is all around the building so that other students and teachers can have a chance to read some poetry" (Heard, 1999, p. 23). Post poems in places children stand, stare, and wait—like at the water fountain, on doors, lockers, at entrances, etc. When it's time to take down a poem and replace it with a new one, the "old" poems can be compiled into an anthology to revisit in book form. Surrounding children with poetry in these incidental ways shows children we value poetry as an everyday part of life.

Juan Felipe Herrera

JUAN FELIPE HERRERA'S BIO

Juan Herrera was born in Fowler, California, on December 27, 1948, an only child of migrant workers from Mexico. Herrera's family finally settled in San Diego, but his early mobile life greatly affected his writing. Herrera attended the University of California where he earned a bachelor's degree in social anthropology. He also earned a Master of Arts degree from Stanford University and a Master of Fine Arts degree from the University of Iowa Writer's Workshop. He has been an educator, writer, performer, musician, and editor and is currently a faculty member at the University of California in Riverside in the Tomás Rivera endowed chair in creative writing. He is married and has five children.

JUAN FELIPE HERRERA'S POETRY

Juan Felipe Herrera has written many works of poetry for both children and adults. His writing for young people has won a lot of recognition including the Ezra Jack Keats Award for *Calling The Doves*, the Americas Award for *Crashboomlove*, and a Pura Belpré honor award for *Laughing Out Loud, I Fly*. He also wrote *Upside Down Boy*, which was adapted into a musical in New York.

Juan Felipe Herrera's bilingual book, *Calling the Doves/El Canto De Las Palomas* (Children's Book Press, 2001) is a poetic picture book memoir about growing up in a migrant farmworker family. As in Pat Mora's story of *Tomas and the Library Lady* (Knopf, 1997), family love and storytelling/poetry traditions are highlighted. Then in Herrera's sequel, *The Upside Down Boy / El niño de cabeza* (Children's Book Press, 2000) we follow the young boy's adjustment to school. This time, a sensitive teacher helps pave the way. Consider Jane Medina's poetry collections, *My Name Is Jorge: On Both Sides of the River* (Boyds Mills, 1999) and *The Dream on Blanca's Wall* (Boyd's Mills Press, 2004) for further insight on the migrant experience. Or look to Monica Gunning's *America, My New Home* (Boyds Mills Press, 2004) or Janet Wong's *Good Luck Gold* (Simon & Schuster, 1994) or Jorge Argueta's *Movie in My Pillow/Una pelicula en mi almohada* (Children's Book Press, 2001) for other perspectives on cultural adjustment.

Children may also want to check out autobiographical picture books by these folk artists: Carmen Lomas Garza's bilingual books *Family Pictures/Cuadros de familia* (Children's Book Press, 1990) and *In My Family/En mi familia* (Children's Book Press, 1996); George Littlechild's expressive

This Land Is My Land (Children's Book Press, 1993); and Normee Ekoo-miak's bilingual memoir, *Arctic Memories* (Holt, 1988). Invite children to share their own experiences of home, family, or moving through drawing their own autobiographical pictures.

For pre-adolescent readers, Herrera has a bilingual collection of poetry, *Laughing Out Loud, I Fly: Poems in English and Spanish* (HarperCollins, 1998) that describes the tastes, smells, and textures of the world around him. There are many other collections of poetry in both English and Spanish to share, including *My Mexico~Mexico Mio* by Tony Johnston (Putnam, 1996), Lori Carlson's *Cool Salsa* (Holt, 1994), and *Red Hot Salsa* (Holt, 2005), and *The Tree Is Older Than You Are* collected by Naomi Shihab Nye (Simon & Schuster, 1995). In addition, children will enjoy poems that use Spanish words and phrases within the English text, called "codeswitching," such as *Confetti* by Pat Mora (Lee and Low, 1996; also available in Spanish 2006) or *Canto Familiar* by Gary Soto (Harcourt, 1995). Invite any Spanish-speaking children or volunteers to read the Spanish version of the poems so others can hear the poetry in the original language. Children who speak a language other than English may want to try translating one of their favorite English poems into their native language or translating a favorite Spanish (or other language) poem into English to share with the group.

Herrera's diverse talents also include picture storybooks for young readers and verse novels for young adults. His bilingual picture books include *Super Cilantro Girl* (Children's Book Press, 2003) about a girl with imaginary superhero powers who rescues her mom and *Featherless/Desplumado* (Children's Book Press, 2004) about a boy who is unable to walk, but has big dreams. His verse novels for older readers are *Crashboomlove* (University of New Mexico Press, 1999), *Downtown Boy* (Scholastic, 2005), and *Cinnamon Girl: Letters Found Inside a Cereal Box* (Rayo, 2005).

Anna Grossnickle Hines

http://www.aghines.com/

ANNA GROSSNICKLE HINES' BIO

Anna Hines was born on July 13, 1946, in Cincinnati, Ohio. She attended San Fernando State College but received both her bachelor's and master's degrees in human development from Pacific Oaks College in California. She worked as a preschool and third-grade teacher before becoming a full-time writer and illustrator. She is married and is the mother of three daughters. Her hobbies include needlework, quilting, knitting, gardening, and grand-parenting.

Many of Hines' books have appeared on national Notable and "best" lists including, International Reading Association Children's Choice list, National Science Teachers Association Outstanding Science Books for Children, Bank Street College Children's Books of the Year, National Council for the Social Studies Notable Children's Trade Books, National Council of Teachers of English Notable Children's Books, Junior Literary Guide Book-of-the-Month Club selection, and others. Her poetry collection, *Pieces: A Year in Poems and Quilts* received the Lee Bennett Hopkins Award for Children's Poetry.

ANNA GROSSNICKLE HINES' POETRY

Although Anna Grossnickle Hines has authored over 50 picture storybooks for young readers, the focus here is on her poetry books, *Pieces: A Year in Poems & Quilts* (Greenwillow, 2001) and *Winter Lights: A Season in Poems & Quilts* (Greenwillow, 2005). In *Pieces: A Year in Poems & Quilts*, Hines blends a variety of styles of poems and handmade quilts to depict seasonal changes in the weather, animals, gardens, and more in vivid fabric colors and descriptive language. An added touch is an informative appendix explaining Hines' meticulous quilting process. Partner this book with poet Ann Whitford Paul's *Eight Hands Round: A Patchwork Alphabet* (HarperTrophy, 1996) or Jacqueline Woodson's poetic *Show Way* (Putnam, 2005) for more examples of quilt art in books. Children can then work together to create a poem-quilt by patchworking together individual poem pages and drawings into a group project quilt to post and share.

Hines continues using her handmade quilts to illustrate and inspire the poems for her companion book, *Winter Lights*. Here the images and illustrations celebrate the varying kinds of light that brighten this dark time of the year, from candles to moonglow. In addition, winter holidays such as Christmas, the feast of Santa Lucia, Hanukkah, Kwanzaa, and the Chinese, or lunar

New Year are also interwoven throughout the poems and illustrations. Again, Hines includes a helpful "making of" section, complete with photographs. Star shapes based on triangles dominate many of the quilt illustrations, so follow up with an activity challenging children to create individual stars out of triangles of fabric or colored construction paper. They can choose a favorite winter poem or create their own to accompany their stars. Contrast Hines' *Winter Lights* collection with Joan Bransfield Graham's book of concrete poetry, *Flicker Flash* (Houghton Mifflin, 2003), which also looks at light in its many forms and add Valerie Worth's poetry book, *At Christmastime* (HarperCollins, 1992), for more poetic moments of the holiday season.

Mary Ann Hoberman

http://www.maryannhoberman.com/

MARY ANN HOBERMAN'S POETRY

Mary Ann Hoberman's poetry often targets our youngest audience with rhythm and repetition, usually published in picture book form or as "read aloud" rhyming "stories," such as in *You Read to Me, I'll Read to You: Very Short Fairy Tales to Read Together* (Little, Brown, 2004). Other inviting collections include *The Llama Who Had No Pajama: 100 Favorite Poems* (Harcourt, 1998), *Fathers, Mothers, Sisters, Brothers: A Collection of Family Poems* (Little, Brown, 2001), and *My Song is Beautiful: Poems and Pictures in Many Voices* (Little, Brown, 1994).

For one outstanding example of Hoberman's style, look for her poem "Take Sound" which she composed especially for the ceremony at which she was given the National Council of Teachers of English Award for Excellence in Poetry for Children. It also appears in Paul Janeczko's poetry anthology *Seeing the Blue Between* (Candlewick, 2002). Hoberman acknowledges that the poem pays homage to the great children's poet David McCord, the first recipient of the award, and in particular to his poem, "Take Sky," by echoing its title and cadence. It focuses on the pleasures of sharing the sounds and words of poetry with children and is a great way to begin a poetry lesson or unit. Combine it with other poems that attempt to "define" poetry like Eve Merriam's "The Poem as a Door" from *The Singing Green* (Morrow, 1992) or "The Bridge" by Kaissar Afif from *The Space Between our Footsteps* (Simon & Schuster, 1998) collected by Naomi Shihab Nye. Challenge children to come up with their own definition of what poetry is to them. Compile these to create a "dictionary" of poetry.

One of Hoberman's most widely anthologized poems is "Brother" from *The Llama Who Had No Pajama*, about an older sibling who wants to give away an annoying little brother. Pair this with Shel Silverstein's "For Sale" poem from *Where the Sidewalk Ends* (Harper & Row, 1974/2004). With their strong rhyme and rhythm, children will enjoy reading these poems out loud. Follow up with Hoberman's poem "O is Open" (from *The Llama Who Had No Pajama*) and make necklaces out of O-shaped cereal (like Cheerios) just for fun. Match these poems with the picture book, *What the No-Good Baby Is Good for* (Putnam, 2005) by Elise Broach and follow up with more of Hoberman's poems from *Fathers, Mothers, Sisters, Brothers: A Collection of Family Poems* (Little, Brown, 2001), and Eve Merriam's *You Be Good and I'll Be Night: Jump On The Bed Poems* (Turtleback, 1994). Begin and end the activity with Hoberman's first and last poems in *The Llama Who Had No Pajama*—"Hello and Good-by" and "Good Morning When It's Morning."

Mary Ann Hoberman has also created a blend of narrative and poetry in her *You Read to Me, I'll Read to You* books of stories, fairy tales, and Mother Goose. Each collection is told in rhyme with columns of color-coded text for two readers to share. The strong rhythms of her poetry serve these simple narratives well. Kids can't resist the back and forth bounce of these two-page tales, so cleverly illustrated by Michael Emberley. These are perfect for parent–child reading activities or for older and younger children to read together.

Sara Holbrook

http://www.saraholbrook.com/

SARA HOLBROOK'S BIO

Sara Holbrook was born on September 15, 1949, and grew up in Berkley, Michigan near Detroit. She earned a bachelor's degree in English and journalism at Mount Union College in Ohio and was the editor of her college newspaper. She added a degree in secondary English education, working part-time as a high school teacher. She later worked in corporate communications, in the field of law, public housing, and as a substance-abuse educator. She is a frequent speaker, presenter, and poetry performer at schools, professional development workshops, and conferences. Sara lives in Ohio, where she enjoys walking the banks of Lake Erie, bike-riding, gardening, swimming, and cooking for family and friends. She has two grown daughters, Katie and Kelly and six grandchildren who provide fresh inspiration.

SARA HOLBROOK'S POETRY

Sara Holbrook began writing poetry when her daughters were small and her first poetry performance audience was one of their slumber parties. Since then she continues to write poetry that particularly focuses on teen and "tween" concerns. In addition, her emphasis on performing poetry has led her to write books about this process for both children and adults with an emphasis on how poetry can be a vehicle for learning across the curriculum.

Few poets address the emotional roller coaster of the tween years better than Sara Holbrook with her poetry collections:

Nothing's the End of the World (Boyds Mills Press, 1995)

I Never Said I Wasn't Difficult (Boyds Mills Press, 1996)

Am I Naturally This Crazy? (Boyds Mills Press, 1996)

Which Way to the Dragon!: Poems for the Coming-On-Strong (Boyds Mills Press, 1996)

The Dog Ate My Homework (Boyds Mills Press, 1997)

Walking on the Boundaries of Change: Poems of Transition (Boyds Mills Press, 1998)

By Definition: Poems Of Feelings (Boyds Mills Press, 2003)

Holbrook's poems are direct and wry snapshots of emotions and experiences that children can relate to. In addition, she employs a variety of poetic forms, both rhyming and unrhyming. Other poets with similar approaches include Judith Viorst in *If I Were in Charge of the World and Other Worries* (Simon & Schuster, 1981), Nikki Grimes in *A Dime a Dozen* (Dial, 1998), and Kristine O'Connell George in *Swimming Upstream: Middle School Poems* (Clarion, 2002). Her work can also serve as an engaging introduction for novels with a similar droll tone, such as Christopher Paul Curtis' novel, *Bud, Not Buddy* (Yearling, 2002)—the perfect match for Holbrook's poem, "Blueprints?" (from *Am I Naturally This Crazy?* Boyds Mills Press, 1996).

Sara Holbrook is also a big advocate of sharing poetry out loud with children, even inviting them to perform it dramatically. Many of her works have a strong voice or structure which lends itself to child performance. In her poem "Copycat," for example, the lines of the poem sound just like two groups of children mimicking each other, by repeating what each other says. It is the perfect poem to read out loud antiphonally in two groups, call-and-response style. Or in other cases, the regular meter of her poems means they can also be adapted to familiar song tunes for singing. While not a particularly complex method of poetry performance, it is an irresistibly fun approach, matching poems to song tunes that contain the same meter. It seems to be most effective with tunes that have a strong, rhythmic beat such as "Row, Row, Row Your Boat" or "Mary Had A Little Lamb" and poems that are very rhythmic. "The Dog Ate My Homework" by Sara Holbrook is fun to sing to the tune of "On Top of Old Smoky." The appeal of music is undeniable, and this musical connection with poetry makes these poems especially memorable.

Holbrook also provides helpful guidelines for staging poems in a variety of ways including hosting contests and competitions in her book for kids, *Wham! It's a Poetry Jam: Discovering Performance Poetry* (Boyds Mills Press, 2002). These spoken word events allow children to participate with the support of a partner or group and help them gain confidence as they share poetry with an audience. Holbrook reminds us to "Show the world that poetry was never meant to simply lie quietly on the page, any more than kids were meant to sit quietly in their seats to read it." For adults who work with children, Holbrook has coauthored with Michael Salinger the excellent resource tool, *Outspoken! How to Improve Writing and Speaking Skills through Poetry Performance* (Heinemann, 2006). And for strategies for connecting poetry with each of the major curricular areas (math, science, and social studies), check out Holbrook's *Practical Poetry; A Nonstandard Approach to Meeting Content-Area Standards* (Heinemann, 2005).

Lee Bennett Hopkins

LEE BENNETT HOPKINS' POETRY

There are several anthologists who have established excellent reputations for compiling numerous high quality collections of poetry for children. Lee Bennett Hopkins may be the most prolific of all, with over 100 books of poetry to his credit as both an anthologist and as a writer. Hopkins has also nurtured many new talents in poetry, commissioning up-and-coming poets to write poems for anthologies he compiles. A few of his most popular titles include *Good Books, Good Times* (HarperTrophy, 2000), *Spectacular Science: A Book of Poems* (Simon & Schuster, 1999), *Opening Days: Sports Poems* (Harcourt, 1996), *School Supplies: A Book of Poems* (Simon & Schuster, 1996), *My America: A Poetry Atlas of the United States* (Simon & Schuster, 2000) and *Days to Celebrate: A Full Year of Poetry, People, Holidays, History, Fascinating Facts, and More* (HarperCollins, 2005) Indeed, as children pore over the dozens of Hopkins anthologies available, they may be inspired to create their own anthologies and even "commission" poems by their favorite friend poets.

Hopkins' work can be an ideal jumping off point for launching a celebration of poetry with one of his collections about books, reading, language, or writing. *Good Books, Good Times* (HarperTrophy, 1990) is one popular example. What teacher, parent, or librarian doesn't relish emphasizing the joys of reading for children who are still learning the process? This thematic collection is organized around that topic, and it includes Hopkins' own oft-shared poem "Good Books, Good Times." Other parallel Hopkins anthologies include *Good Rhymes, Good Times* (HarperTrophy, 2000) and *Wonderful Words: Poems About Reading, Writing, Speaking, and Listening* (Simon & Schuster, 2004). Also look for Mary Perrotta Rich's compilation of the bookmark poems composed in celebration of National Children's Book Week each year and gathered in the collection, *Book Poems: Poems from National Children's Book Week, 1959–1998* (Children's Book Council, 1998). Children may want to create their own bookmarks with their favorite or original poem about books and reading on them.

Teachers and librarians find Hopkins' work helpful because so many of his anthologies are organized around themes or topics that lend themselves to teaching school subject areas. For example, *Hand in Hand: An American History through Poetry* (Simon & Schuster, 1994) offers a chronological view of American history through poetry. Combine this with the individual experience found in Joyce Carol Thomas' *I Have Heard of a Land* (HarperCollins, 1995) or one family's history in Ann Turner's *Mississippi Mud* (Harper-Collins, 1997). Or try Hopkins' collection, *Spectacular Science* (Simon & Schuster, 1999) which includes science-related poems by writers from Carl Sandburg to Rebecca Kai Dotlich. Children will appreciate both the contextualized vocabulary and the clear imagery found in poems like "What is Science?" by Dotlich. *Marvelous Math* (Simon & Schuster, 1997) includes math-related poems by an assortment of poets, like "Take a Number" by Mary O'Neill. These poems can help clarify terms and concepts, as well as add fun and enrichment to math lessons or tutoring.

We can also pair Hopkins' thematic collections with fiction or nonfiction books on the same topic for added breadth. For example, link Hopkins' anthology, *It's About Time* (Simon & Schuster, 1993) with Kathryn Lasky's picture book biography, *The Man Who Made Time Travel* (Farrar, Straus & Giroux, 2003). Children can study how time is measured by scientists versus poets or assemble a collection of various timepieces and measurement devices along with their favorite "time for poetry" poems.

Lee Bennett Hopkins has also authored biographical and autobiographical writings. Two books about his own life and work include *Writing Bug* (Richard C. Owen, 1993) and *Been To Yesterdays: Poems Of A Life* (Wordsong/Boyds Mills Press, 1995) told through poems. Two collections about poets and poetry teaching include *Pass the Poetry Please* (Harper-Collins, 1986) and *Pauses; Autobiographical Reflections of 101 Creators of Children's Books* (HarperCollins, 1995). His advice to adults who share poetry with children is simple, but powerful: "Don't dissect poetry, enjoy it … everyday! There shouldn't be a day without poetry—it fits into every area of the curriculum, every area of life."

Paul B. Janeczko

http://www.pauljaneczko.com/

PAUL JANECZKO'S BIO

Paul Janeczko was born on July 27, 1945, in Passaic, New Jersey. He earned a bachelor's degree from St. Francis College in Biddeford, Maine, and a master's degree from John Carroll University in Ohio. He was an English teacher in Ohio, Massachusetts, and Maine for many years. He began compiling poem anthologies for his students which led to more formal publication of many, many anthologies, as well as poetry of his own. He has also written teaching guides for using poetry and poetry writing in the classroom and is now a frequent speaker and workshop leader. His hobbies include running, biking, swimming, cooking vegetarian meals, playing 5-string banjo, and working with wood. He is married and has a daughter.

Janeczko's work has been recognized with many awards and "best" list citations, including the American Library Association Books for Young Adults, American Library Association Notable Books, New York Public Library Best Books, *School Library Journal* Best Young Adult Books of the Year, among others.

PAUL JANECZKO'S POETRY

Paul Janeczko has created many appealing anthologies of poetry for young people such as *Dirty Laundry Pile: Poems in Different Voices* (Harper-Collins, 2001), *Very Best (Almost) Friends: A Collection of Friendship Poetry* (Candlewick, 1998), and *Hey, You! Poems to Skyscrapers, Mosquitoes, and Other Fun Things* (HarperCollins, 2007), as well as authoring several of his own original poetry books such as *That Sweet Diamond: Baseball Poems* (Atheneum, 1998), *Stardust otel* (Scholastic, 1993), *Brickyard Summer* (Orchard, 1989) and *Worlds Afire* (Candlewick, 2004). Several of his anthologies for children gather poems based on unique themes particular to poetic form, from concrete poetry to haiku including:

Poetry from A to Z: A Guide to Young Writers (Bradbury, 1994)

A Kick in the Head: An Everyday Guide to Poetic Forms (Candlewick, 2005)

A Poke in the I: A Collection of Concrete Poems (Candlewick, 2001)

Wing Nuts: Screwy Haiku with J. Patrick Lewis (Little, Brown, 2006)

Stone Bench in an Empty Park (Orchard Books, 2000)

Paul Janeczko has a wonderful resource book for both children and young adults filled with serious and wacky poetry forms in *Poetry from A to Z; A Guide for Young Writers*, including clerihews, how-to poems, letter poems, and others. Partner this book with Avis Harley's alphabet of poetry: *Fly with Poetry; An ABC of Poetry* (Wordsong/Boyds Mills Press, 2000) and *Leap into Poetry: More ABCs of Poetry* (Wordsong/Boyds Mills Press, 2001). Children may enjoy discovering unusual forms of poetry or even trying their hands at writing them. Or working as a group, children can create their own alphabet book of poetry with each child responsible for a letter to build a poem upon. Other Janeczko anthologies that offer additional guidance to budding poets include *Seeing the Blue Between: Advice and Inspirations for Young Poets* (Candlewick, 2002), *The Place My Words Are Looking for: What Poets Say About and through Their Work* (Bradbury, 1990), and *Poetspeak: In Their Work, About Their Work: A Selection* (Bradbury, 1983).

In his picture book guide to poetic form, *A Kick in the Head: An Everyday Guide to Poetic Forms* children will encounter examples of 29 different kinds of poems from tankas to pantoums accompanied by Chris Raschka's ebullient illustrations. Older children may enjoy reading poet Helen Frost's work which also showcases several different distinctive poetic forms such as the sestina, sonnet, pantoum, acrostic, and haiku in *Spinning through the Universe: A Novel in Poems from Room 214* (Farrar, Straus & Giroux, 2004).

Janeczko and Raschka also paired up to create *A Poke in the I: A Collection of Concrete Poems*, an inviting introduction to "shape" poetry. Children typically enjoy the poet's creative use of the physical shape of the subject of the poem to convey meaning. It's a poetic form they like imitating and experimenting with. They can take a favorite poem and arrange the words in the shape of the poem subject or create new, original shape poems. Follow up with other models of concrete or "shape" poetry including Joan Bransfield Graham's books, *Flicker Flash* (Houghton Mifflin, 1999) and *Splish Splash* (Houghton Mifflin, 1994), J. Patrick Lewis's *Doodle Dandies: Poems that Take Shape* (Atheneum, 1998), Heidi Roemer's *Come to My Party* (Holt, 2004), and John Grandits' *Technically, It's Not My Fault: Concrete Poems* (Clarion, 2004).

Paul Janeczko incorporates haiku in many of his books and anthologies, a popular form for classroom instruction. His collaboration with J. Patrick Lewis, *Wing Nuts: Screwy Haiku* weaves humorous haiku into a story frame, and his picture book anthology, *Stone Bench in an Empty Park*, contains "urban" haiku alongside black and white photographs of city scenes. Add the animal haiku of Jack Prelutsky in *If Not for the Cat: Haiku* (Greenwillow,

2004) and the haiku-biography, *Cool Melons Turn to Frogs: The Life and Poems of Issa*, by Matthew Gollub (Lee & Low Books, 1998) for more varied perspectives on this ancient Japanese form of poetry. With these examples of the 17-syllable form of poetry under their belts, children may want to try creating their own.

Bobbi Katz

http://www.bobbikatz.com/

BOBBI KATZ'S BIO

Bobbi Katz was born on May 2, 1933, in Newburgh, New York. She graduated from Goucher College and studied at Hebrew University of Jerusalem. She was married and has two children. She is also a peace and environmental activist.

Katz's first job was as a freelance writer and editor of *Middle Eastern Affairs*. During her varied career, she has worked as a social worker, an art historian, a fashion editor, a radio talk host, a program director for an arts council, a college creative writing teacher, and as an editor of educational books. Best known for children's poetry, Katz also writes biographies, essays, and picture books. Her honors include *Booklist* Top Ten Poetry Pick, *Kirkus* Starred Review, National Council of Teachers of English Notable Book.

BOBBI KATZ'S POETRY

Bobbi Katz has created anthologies of poems by many writers such as the popular *Pocket Poems* (Dutton, 2004), as well as collections of her own original poetry, including *A Rumpus of Rhymes: A Book of Noisy Poems* (Dutton, 2001), *Truck Talk: Rhymes on Wheels* (Cartwheel, 1997), *Once Around The Sun* (Harcourt Books, 2006), and *We, the People* (Greenwillow, 2000).

With *Pocket Poems*, Bobbi Katz has assembled a collection of over 50 short, lively poems by a wide array of authors from Mother Goose to Jack Prelutsky that are perfect for reading aloud with with young children. It's an appealing compilation to connect with Lee Bennett Hopkins' anthology *Climb into My Lap: First Poems to Read Together* (Simon & Schuster, 1998), or Jack Prelutsky's "American Mother Goose" rhymes in *Ride a Purple Pelican* (Greenwillow, 1986), or Mary Ann Hoberman's inviting verse in *The Llama Who Had No Pajama: 100 Favorite Poems* (Harcourt, 1998). Since these are pocket-sized poems, children can decorate a fabric or paper pocket and tuck a copy of their favorite poem inside for sharing again at home.

In *A Rumpus Of Rhymes: A Book of Noisy Poems* (Dutton, 2001), Katz's own original poems are full of onomatopoeia and sound play. Plus, typeface and font are used very creatively to suggest sound, volume, and movement, much like Karla Kuskin's classic, *Roar and More* (Boyds Mills Press, 2004). Children may want to imitate this format by using font size creatively in copying or creating their own poems. They will also enjoy Rebecca Kai

Dotlich's *Over in the Pink House: New Jump Rope Rhymes* (Boyds Mills Press, 2004), a collection of original jump rope rhymes for chanting out loud. Invite the children outdoors for poem chanting, jumping rope, and other noisy activities.

It may be surprising to find a book of poetry on the subject of trucks, but Bobbi Katz has authored just such a collection, *Truck Talk: Rhymes on Wheels* (Cartwheel, 1997). She includes inviting color photographs of tow trucks, ambulances, garbage trucks, and more, along with short poems from the perspective of each truck. Truck-lovers will enjoy comparing this with the nonfiction picture book, *Seymour Simon's Book of Trucks* (HarperTrophy, 2002) or with the poem picture book, *Truck Song* by Diane Siebert (HarperTrophy, 1987). Invite the children to bring toy trucks to loan in creating a truck poetry display.

Poetry that celebrates the months of the year is a natural for sharing with kids who are so attuned to the school schedule, the next holiday, and the change of the seasons. In *Once Around the Sun* (Harcourt, 2006), Katz has created a picture book with a poem for each month that celebrates child activities at home and at school. For more calendar-focused poetry books, look for *July is a Mad Mosquito* by J. Patrick Lewis (Atheneum, 1994), *Turtle in July* by Marilyn Singer (Macmillan, 1989), and Francisco X. Alarcon's series of four books focusing on the four seasons of the year, called "The Magical Cycle of the Seasons" series (Children's Book Press). For a fun follow-up activity, recycle old calendars by covering up the page of old dates for each month with a poem that suits the photograph or illustration provided for each month.

For older children, Bobbi Katz has authored a collection of poetry that is ideal for sharing in the social studies entitled *We, the People* (Greenwillow, 2000). Katz has done extensive research to create a series of first-person poems that work as character sketches of famous and ordinary Americans from colonial times through the present day. The poems lend themselves to dramatic read aloud (in costume) and can be paired with book-length biographies of the poem's subjects. For more such poem biographies, seek out Lee Bennett Hopkins' *Lives: Poems about Famous Americans* (Harper-Collins, 1999), J. Patrick Lewis' *Heroes and She-Roes: Poems of Amazing and Everyday Heroes* (Dial, 2005), and Carole Boston Weatherford's *Remember the Bridge: Poems of a People* (Philomel, 2002). Children can work together to make a poem timeline, placing their favorite poems in chronological order based on the subject's place in history.

Finally, Katz has also written helpful professional materials for teachers and librarians that support developing effective poetry lessons, including *25 Great Grammar Poems with Activities* (Scholastic, 2000) and *Poems Just for Us! With Cross-Curriculum Activities* (Scholastic, 1996).

X. J. Kennedy

http://www.xjanddorothymkennedy.com

X. J. KENNEDY'S BIO

X. J. Kennedy (Joseph Kennedy, known as Joe) was born on August 21, 1929, in Dover, New Jersey. He earned his bachelor's degree from Seton Hall University, a master's degree from Columbia University, a "certificat" from the University of Paris, and complete additional graduate studies at the University of Michigan where he was a teaching fellow. Kennedy also received an honorary doctorate from Adelphi University. He has taught English at several colleges and universities, including an extensive tenure at Tufts University. He also served in the United States Navy as a journalist. He is married to writer Dorothy Kennedy and they have five children.

Kennedy has gained much recognition for his writing of poetry for both adults and children, including a National Council on the Arts and Humanities grant, a Guggenheim fellowship, many *New York Times Book Review* Outstanding Book of the Year citations, multiple National Council of Teachers of English Notable book citations, several *School Library Journal* Best Book of the Year recognitions and American Library Association Notable Book citations, Bank Street College Best Children's Book of the Year, numerous New York Public Library 100 Best Books of the Year citations, *Booklist* Editors' Choice, International Reading Association and Children's Book Council Children's Choice citation, *Horn Book* Fanfare list, *Parenting* magazine Award for Excellence in Children's Literature, and others. He was honored with the National Council for Teachers of English Award for Excellence in Children's Poetry for a lifetime of writing for children.

X. J. KENNEDY'S POETRY

X. J. Kennedy is a highly regarded writer of poetry for adults, as well as for children. In addition, he has collaborated with his wife, Dorothy, herself an English scholar, on two award-winning books for children, *Talking Like the Rain* (Little, Brown, 1992) and *Knock at a Star: A Child's Introduction to Poetry* (Little, Brown, 1999). On her own, she has also published several poetry anthologies for children including *I Thought I'd Take My Rat to School* (Little, Brown, 1993) and *Make Things Fly* (McElderry, 1998). They have each authored college textbooks on writing, too.

X. J. Kennedy is known for his playful sense of humor, love of strong meter, and witty wordplay. His collection, *Exploding Gravy, Poems to Make You Laugh* (Little, Brown, 2002) is a compilation of a quarter century of some of his most humorous poems. One favorite example is "Italian Noodles," in which Kennedy coins new words to rhyme with noodle names. For example, the speaker in the poem eats ravioli "sloli" and is hungry for "spaghetti" "alretti." It's a fun poem to read out loud with a different group for each stanza. Then identify and discuss the "made up" words and brainstorm other possibilities for rhymes for "linguine" or "macaroni" or "vermicelli," etc. And of course, bring examples of different kinds of raw pasta and make pasta poem art. For similar light-hearted poetry, children can check out the work of Jack Prelutsky, John Ciardi, and Mary Ann Hoberman.

Kennedy's book, *Knock at a Star: A Child's Introduction to Poetry*, a collaboration with his wife is an engaging invitation to the elements of poetry as well as nearly 200 poems. It is considered a standard, part poetry, part instructional guide alongside such titles as Paul Janeczko's excellent "guide books" for aspiring poets, such as *Seeing the Blue Between* (Candlewick, 2002), Bernice Cullinan's *A Jar of Tiny Stars: Poems by NCTE Award-winning Poets* (Boyds Mills Press, 1996), or Myra Cohn Livingston's *Climb into the Bell Tower: Essays on Poetry* (Harper, 1990).

Younger children will enjoy Kennedy's poem picture books, *Elympics* (Philomel, 1999) and *Elefantina's Dream* (Philomel, 2002) which have a gentler humor with a focus on amusing elephant characters. Kennedy's clever use of language will also appeal to the older reader, who will "catch" the puns and plays on words, as when an elephant character wins "by a nose!" This is a fun and appealing introduction to the Olympic traditions (Summer games, Winter games, gold medals, etc.), as well as to the sly and humorous style of X. J. Kennedy. Follow up with a nonfiction book from the *Eyewitness* series, *Olympics* (Knopf, 1999) for factual information about the Olympic Games, the Paralympics, as well as the tools and techniques for considering Olympic-level competition. Plan a Poetry Olympics with children deciding on gold, silver, and bronze medal distinctions for their favorite poems in the categories of humor, nature, school, sports, history, multicultural poems, etc.

Karla Kuskin

KARLA KUSKIN'S BIO

Karla Kuskin was born on July 17, 1932, in New York City. Encouraged by her parents and teachers, Kuskin began writing poetry as a young girl. She attended Antioch College and earned a bachelor's of fine arts degree from Yale University. She is married and has two grown children who are photographers.

Karla Kuskin's first book developed from her senior thesis. *Roar and More*, a children's book she wrote and designed, was published in 1956, in a slightly altered form. Kuskin has gone on to become a prolific writer and illustrator of over 50 works of children's poetry, storybooks in verse, easy readers, and even nonfiction. Her many awards include American Institute of Graphic Arts Book Show awards, American Library Association Notables, International Reading Association Children's Choice distinctions, a National Book Award nomination, and the National Council of Teachers of English Award for Excellence in Poetry for Children award given for a poet's entire body of work. Incidentally, Karla Kuskin also created the art for the medallion of the NCTE Excellence in Poetry for Children Award.

KARLA KUSKIN'S POETRY

Karla Kuskin's pictures and poetry are brimming over with the experiences of children growing up in a big city. For a wonderful compilation of poems from several previous works as well as new poems, look for *Moon, Have You Met My Mother? The Collected Poems of Karla Kuskin* (HarperCollins, 2003). But Kuskin also has many outstanding previous volumes of poetry worth seeking out such as *Dogs and Dragons, Trees and Dreams: A Collection of Poems* (HarperCollins, 1980), which includes some of her best known poems such as "Bugs," "Write about a Radish," "I Woke up This Morning," and "Hughbert and the Glue." The book also includes brief introductions in italics above the titles of many poems offering sage advice for the aspiring writer. Delicate ink sketches by Kuskin herself appear strategically on the line that underlines each poem's title. Other poets who provide a bit of insight into their own writing processes with explanations accompanying their poems include Gary Soto (*A Fire in My Hands*, Harcourt, 2006), Eloise Greenfield (*In the Land of Words*, HarperCollins, 2004) and the collected poets in many of Paul Janeczko's anthologies (*Seeing the Blue Between*, Candlewick, 2002; *The Place My Words are Looking For*, Bradbury, 1990). These are wonderful resources for children who are curious about where a poet gets ideas for a poem and how they begin to write poetry. Kuskin shares further insights in her autobiographical picture book, *Thoughts, Pictures, and Words* (Richard C. Owen, 1995).

Many of Kuskin's poems have a strong voice or distinctive structure that lends itself to being read aloud and performing chorally. For example, try "The Question" (*Dogs and Dragons*), a poem that poses multiple answers to the question, "What do you want to be when you grow up?" Different groups or individual children can each pipe in with a different answer from the poem, "I think I'd like to be the sky," "Or maybe I will stay a child," etc. Kuskin also has written many poems for children that incorporate a linear format that lends itself to line-around reading. For example, look for "Rules" (*Dogs and Dragons*), a listing of "rules" such as "Do not jump on ancient uncles" that children will find hilarious. And of course they may want to generate their own list of crazy rules to follow.

Or poems with a repeated word can be read aloud using the word as a kind of chorus for group participation. Karla Kuskin's poem, "Snow" portrays a traditional picture of winter's snow moments using the word "snow" many times throughout the poem. However, in this case the designated word occurs in various places in the lines of the poem, sometimes as part of a compound word. Thus the read aloud can be somewhat chaotic at first, but is lots of fun. And for children, who don't live in snowy climates, incorporate Frank Asch's poem, "Sunflakes" (*Ring Out, Wild Bells: Poems about Holidays and Seasons*, Harcourt 1992, collected by Lee Bennett Hopkins) which imagines snowy traditions in sunny weather with cleverly coined words such as "sunman" and "sunball." Follow up with art activities using white snowball-shaped circles or yellow sun-shaped circles to create scenes and characters to accompany the poems.

Another good poem to share is "Three Wishes" (*Near the Window Tree*, HarperCollins, 1975) since nearly every child has wished for wishes. This poem begins, "Three wishes/Three. /The first/A tree," and then goes on to itemize three wishes for a happy afternoon: a tree, a chair, and a book. Read this out loud while seated in a chair near a window with a view of a tree, if possible. Then invite the children to find their own wished-for books and comfortable reading spots.

Kuskin's poetry can also be connected with works of fiction and non-fiction for added enrichment. For example, the title poem from *Moon, Have You Met My Mother? The Collected Poems of Karla Kuskin* (HarperCollins, 2003) is a lovely match for Kevin Henkes' Caldecott award winning picture book, *Kitten's First Full Moon* (Greenwillow, 2004) or even for the simple nonfiction story, *Man on the Moon* (Viking, 1997) by Anastasia Suen. For a more rambunctious example, share "I Woke Up This Morning" (*Dogs and Dragons*) and begin with a soft voice reading aloud gradually getting louder as the poem builds momentum (and the fonts increase in size in the poem's text). It's the perfect follow up to a read aloud of Judith Viorst's classic picture book, *Alexander and the Terrible, Horrible, No Good, Very Bad Day* (Aladdin, 1987). Children who enjoy Kuskin's poetry may also want to seek out the work of poets Marilyn Singer, Deborah Chandra, and David McCord.

Dennis Lee

http://www.library.utoronto.ca/canpoetry/lee/

DENNIS LEE'S BIO

Dennis Lee was born August 31, 1939 in Toronto, Ontario, Canada. Lee graduated from the University of Toronto earning both a bachelor's and a master's degree. During his career he has worked as a lecturer in English, as an editorial consultant, poetry editor, as the cofounder and editor of the House of Anansi Press in Toronto, and as a lyricist for the TV series "Fraggle Rock." He contributed to the scripts for the films, "The Dark Crystal" and "Labyrinth." Dennis Lee also holds an honorary doctorate from Trent University. He enjoys crossword puzzles, jazz and blues, art by Cezanne, Pollock and Rothko, and cello music. He is married and has three grown children.

Lee is widely regarded as Canada's best-loved children's poet and his work has garnered many awards including the Governor General's Award for Poetry, Canadian Association of Children's Librarians Best Book Medals, Hans Christian Andersen Honour List citation, Canadian Library Association Award, and Canadian Library Association Book of the Year for Children nomination. Lee's manuscripts and papers are in a permanent collection at the Fisher Rare Book Room at the University of Toronto.

DENNIS LEE'S POETRY

The writing of Canadian poet Dennis Lee is often compared to that of Shel Silverstein or Jack Prelutsky because of his zany humor, strong rhythm, and child-friendly topics. Although he may not be as familiar to audiences in the United States, his work still holds wide appeal. In addition, he incorporates many uniquely Canadian references in his verses, easily understandable in context, but offering an added layer of richness to the poems—much like the use of Spanish words in the poems of Gary Soto or Pat Mora.

Look for Lee's collection, *The Ice Cream Store* (HarperCollins, 1999), full of inventive, energetic, and off-the-wall humor. From the title poem on, he celebrates the diversity of children comparing them to ice cream flavors such as chocolate, vanilla, and maple. His rhythmical poems invite children to read or sing along. Take his poem, "A Home Like a Hiccup," for example, that asks children to speculate about what they would be like if they had been born in a different place, and then provides a litany of place names that are fun to pronounce, "*Like Minsk! or Omsk! or Tomsk! or Bratsk!*" In the end, however, there's no place like home, and children can provide the name of their individual hometowns when the last line is read aloud, "So the name of MY place is _____." Invite the children to locate the poem places on a map or mark the places that they were born or have lived.

Dennis Lee's poetry book, *Bubblegum Delicious* (HarperCollins, 2001) is grounded in the rhythms of childhood playground rhymes and is a natural companion to Judy Sierra's *Schoolyard Rhymes: Kids' Own Rhymes for Rope Skipping, Hand Clapping, Ball Bouncing, and Just Plain Fun* (Knopf, 2005) or the sing-along rhymes of Alan Katz in *Take Me Out of the Bathtub* (McElderry, 2001). Gather or make simple homemade musical instruments (tambourine, jingle bells, drums) and invite the children to play and sing along with the poems, rhymes, and songs.

Other appealing collections of Dennis Lee's poetry can be found in *Garbage Delight: Another Helping* (Key Porter, 2002) and *Alligator Pie* (Key Porter, 2001). Compare the title poem "Garbage Delight" to Shel Silverstein's "Sarah Cynthia Sylvia Stout Would Not Take the Garbage Out" from *Where the Sidewalk Ends* (HarperCollins, 1974). Many of the most popular poems from these anthologies and other Lee collections were chosen by Jack Prelutsky for an anthology of Dennis Lee's work published in the U.S., entitled, *Dinosaur Dinner (with a Slice of Alligator Pie)* (Random House, 1997). Look for the fun poem about a creature named an "Ookpik" and read it echo style, with the children repeating each line. Provide children with a clothespin and yarn to create their own Ookpik creatures. They can then write their own Ookpik couplets and compose a group poem together.

Constance Levy

CONSTANCE LEVY'S BIO

Constance Levy was born on May 8, 1931, in St. Louis, Missouri. She received both her bachelor's and her master's degrees from Washington University in St. Louis. Levy worked for many years as an elementary school teacher in Missouri, then as a children's poet as part of the Writers in the Schools Program for seven years, and is now a frequent speaker at schools and educational conferences. She was married and has four children and lives in St. Louis, Missouri. She enjoys exercising, taking walks, cooking, and entertaining her family.

Constance Levy has won many honors including Bank Street College's Children's Book of the Year, *Boston Globe Horn Book* Honor Award, American Booksellers Pick of the List, several National Council of Teachers of English Notable Book in Language Arts citations, New York Library's Select 100 Titles for Children's Books and the Lee Bennett Hopkins Award for the best poetry book of the year for *Splash! Poems of our Watery World*.

CONSTANCE LEVY'S POETRY

Many of Constance Levy's poems use "nature" as a theme and depict everything from butterflies to weeds with a sense of wonder and playfulness. Her poetry collections include:

I'm Going to Pet a Worm Today and Other Poems (McElderry, 1991)

A Tree Place and Other Poems (McElderry, 1994)

When Whales Exhale and Other Poems (McElderry, 1996)

A Crack in the Clouds and Other Poems (McElderry, 1998)

Splash! Poems of Our Watery World (Orchard, 2002)

So many of Levy's poems link beautifully with picture books of fiction and nonfiction. Their directness and effective use of first person or question/answer format invite engagement and interaction. For example, her collection, *A Crack in the Clouds*, includes a gamut of "cloud" poems that convey the awe and adventure experienced by Lindbergh in the first transatlantic flight in *Flight: The Journey of Charles Lindbergh* by Robert Burleigh (Philomel, 1991). Gather other factual books about flight and airplanes (such as Seymour Simon's *The Paper Airplane Book*, Puffin 1976) and invite the children to create displays of clouds, paper planes, and matching poems. For younger children, take a step outside to look at real clouds and share the classic picture book, *It Looked Like Spilt Milk* by Charles Shaw (HarperCollins, 1988). Read aloud some of Levy's cloud poems and then have students tear white paper into corresponding cloud images and mount them on blue paper—imitating the illustrations of Shaw's book.

The poems in her award winning collection, *Splash! Poems of our Watery World*, offer a similar smorgasbord of poems, but this time the topic is water in its many forms. Two of the poems, "Flood Line" and "River Games" describe the river as a living thing, almost with a personality. Tie these together with Jane Kurtz's picture book poem, *River Friendly, River Wild* (Simon & Schuster, 2000) about a young girl's ordeal during North Dakota's Red River Valley Flood in 1997. Or children may enjoy connecting Levy's "water" poems with the concrete poetry about water in Joan Bransfield Graham's *Splish Splash* (Houghton Mifflin, 2001). They can try creating their own water, flood, or river poems on shaped paper.

Constance Levy offers more nature poems in *A Tree Place and Other Poems* (McElderry, 1994) and *I'm Going to Pet a Worm Today and Other Poems* (McElderry, 1991). Her style compares nicely with Kristine O'Connell in her poetry collection, *Old Elm Speaks: Tree Poems* (Clarion, 1998) or Aileen Fisher's *Sing of the Earth and Sky: Poems about Our Planet and the Wonders Beyond* (Boyds Mills Press, 2003). For a fun follow-up activity, share "Birdseed Song" from *I'm Going to Pet a Worm Today* and provide materials for making small, individual bird feeders. For example, spread peanut butter on the outside of a pinecone and then roll it in birdseed and hang it outdoors on a string as a homemade bird feeder.

J. Patrick Lewis

http://www.jpatricklewis.com/

J. PATRICK LEWIS' BIO

J. Patrick Lewis and his twin brother were born on May 5, 1942 in Gary, Indiana. Lewis earned his bachelor's degree at St. Joseph's College in Indiana, his master's degree from Indiana University, and his Ph.D. in economics from The Ohio State University. While working on his doctorate, he became an International Research and Exchanges Fellow, and he and his family spent a year in the former USSR. Later, he and his family participated in cultural exchanges, and they returned to Moscow and St. Petersburg for ten shorter visits. For over twenty years, Lewis taught economics at Otterbein College in Westerville, Ohio, retiring in 1998. While teaching, he published widely in academic journals, newspapers, and magazines on the topic of economics.

Lewis then turned to writing children's poetry and took three years to study the craft of poetry on his own. His first book of poems for children, *A Hippopotamusn't*, was published in 1990 and he has followed with nearly 50 more children's books since then, most of which are poetry. Lewis's poetry has been recognized by several American Library Association Notable Children's Book citations, among other honors. Lewis is married and has five children. He is also a contributor of children's book reviews for the *New York Times* and a frequent speaker at schools and conferences.

J. PATRICK LEWIS' POETRY

The themes and subjects of J. Patrick Lewis' poetry collections are incredibly wide-ranging with a frequent focus on science-related and historical topics. In addition, he enjoys experimenting with poetic form and wordplay and has authored everything from narrative poems to concrete poetry to limericks to riddles to haiku. To begin, share Lewis' tribute to the library entitled "Necessary Gardens" (*Please Bury Me in the Library*, Harcourt, 2005), an eight-line acrostic poem with each letter of the word "language" used to begin a line of the poem. After reading the poem aloud once, find eight volunteers, one for each word/line, to "pop up" and read/say each line wherever they are seated. And if children enjoy this acrostic form, challenge them to try writing their own acrostic poems with book-related words of their choice. Look for another Lewis collection of poems about books in *The Bookworm's Feast: A Potluck of Poems* (Dial, 1999) or Lee Bennett Hopkins' anthology, *Good Books, Good Times* (HarperTrophy, 2000).

In the area of social studies, Lewis' work could almost be its own curriculum. One could introduce biography with at least three works by Lewis: *Heroes And She-Roes: Poems Of Amazing And Everyday Heroes* (Dial, 2005), *Vherses: A Celebration Of Outstanding Women* (Creative Editions, 2005), and *Freedom Like Sunlight: Praise Songs for Black Americans* (Creative Editions, 2000). Tackle geography with *A World of Wonders: Geographic Travels in Verse and Rhyme* (Dial Books, 2002), *Monumental Verses* (National Geographic, 2005), and *Castles, Old Stone Poems* (Wordsong/Boyds Mills Press, 2006) coauthored with Rebecca Kai Dotlich. Then link these gems with *Got Geography!* selected by Lee Bennett Hopkins (Greenwillow, 2006) or Diane Siebert's *Tour America : A Journey Through Poems And Art* (Chronicle Books, 2006). Post a world map and locate the settings for each poem. Encourage children to find or create poems for places on the map that are not yet in the books. Check out the poet's own Web site for fun "historical" black and white photos of his own childhood.

There are also excellent choices among his science and math-related poetry books beginning with his first book of poetry ever published, *A Hippopotamustn't: And Other Animal Poems* (Dial, 1990) to later works such as *Scientrickery: Riddles in Science* (Harcourt, 2004) and *Arithme-Tickle: An Even Number of Odd Riddle-Rhymes* (Harcourt, 2002). Look for additional titles of animal poetry by Douglas Florian and Joyce Sidman along with Lee Bennett Hopkins' collections *Spectacular Science* (Simon & Schuster, 1999) and *Marvelous Math* (Simon & Schuster, 1997) to provide a rich science and math library of poetry. Not only are these poems rich in information, but they are playful and humorous and well-suited for reading aloud and performing chorally—in the library or in science class.

Though literary critics would discount books like *The Guinness Book of World Records* as having any literary value at all, such books of trivia, almanacs of facts, and accounts of strange and bizarre occurrences are extremely popular with children, especially boys. J. Patrick Lewis has a wonderful parallel poetry collection to share entitled, *A Burst Of Firsts* (Dial, 2001) which includes both famous accomplishments such as "First Men On The Moon" as well as not so well known feats by the "First Person Who Jumped Rope More Than 14,000 Times in One Hour." Perhaps children will want to glorify their own firsts (first word, first day of school) in poem form or create "found" poems by arranging the words of a Guinness record setting article in list poem format. Lewis' gift for finding poetry in the most unlikely places may motivate even the most reluctant poetry fan.

Myra Cohn Livingston

MYRA COHN LIVINGSTON'S POETRY

Called the "poet's poet," Myra Cohn Livingston's writing is characterized by its elegance and sensitivity and its devotion to form and structure. Although many of her 50+ books are now out of print, they may still be on the library's shelves. She pioneered the creation of thematic anthologies that gathered poems together on current single topics such as holidays, animals, and seasons. These include topical collections of her own original poetry:

A Circle of Seasons (Holiday House, 1982)

Sky Songs (Holiday House, 1984)

Celebrations (Holiday House, 1985)

Earth Songs (Holiday House, 1986)

Sea Songs (Holiday House, 1986)

Space Songs (Holiday House, 1988)

Up in the Air (Holiday House, 1989)

Birthday Poems (Holiday House, 1989)

Festivals (Holiday House, 1996)

Cricket Never Does: A Collection of Haiku and Tanka (McElderry, 1997)

In addition, Livingston compiled several other anthologies with poems by many different poets. These include:

Easter Poems (Holiday House, 1985)

Thanksgiving Poems (Holiday House, 1985)

Poems for Jewish Holidays (Holiday House, 1986)

Valentine Poems (Holiday House, 1987)

Poems for Mothers (Holiday House, 1988)

Poems for Fathers (Holiday House, 1989)

If You Ever Meet a Whale (Holiday House, 1992)

Animal, Vegetable, Mineral: Poems About Small Things (Harper-collins, 1994)

These wonderful collections are examples of what poetry collecting is all about. Children may enjoy assembling their own collections centered on a favorite theme or topic.

Two of Myra Cohn Livingston's particularly enduring poetry collections are *Festivals* and *Celebrations* with vivid full color illustrations by Leonard Everett Fisher. Count on Myra Cohn Livingston for vivid imagery and powerful metaphors. In *Festivals*, she presents both familiar and new celebrations from a variety of cultures including Dia de los Muertos, Tet Nguyen-Dan, and Ramadan. *Celebrations* is one of her most popular collections with a thematic connection that teachers, librarians, and parents can refer to when special occasions and events beg for a particular poem. Connect these with Mary Lankford's nonfiction books for more information about traditions and celebrations around the world, such as *Hopscotch Around the World* (Harper-Collins, 1992) and *Birthdays Around the World* (HarperCollins, 2002). Lee Bennett Hopkins' anthology, *Days to Celebrate: A Full Year of Poetry, People, Holidays, History, Fascinating Facts, and More* (Greenwillow, 2005) can be an additional resource for holiday poetry planning.

Livingston has also authored several important professional resources for adults who work with children including *The Child As Poet: Myth or Reality?* (Horn Book, 1984), *Climb Into The Bell Tower: Essays On Poetry* (Harper, 1990), and *Poem-Making: Ways to Begin Writing Poetry* (Harper, 1991), a book suitable for young people who aspire to be writers, too. For expanding a professional poetry library, seek out similar resource titles by Georgia Heard, Ralph Fletcher, Barbara Esbensen. David Harrison, Sara Holbrook, and Lee Bennett Hopkins.

Michio Mado

MICHIO MADO'S POETRY

Michio Mado's first work translated into English was *The Animals: Selected Poems* (McElderry, 1992) illustrated with exquisite papercut illustrations by award-winning illustrator Mitsumasa Anno. Each poem appears in both Japanese and English, making it an excellent example of bilingual poetry. Contrast this selection with other bilingual poetry such as *Iguanas in the Snow/Iguanas en la nieve.* (Children's Book Press, 2001) by Francisco X. Alarcón or *Maples in the Mist: Poems for Children from the Tang Dynasty* (Lothrop, Lee & Shepard, 1996), Minfong Ho's collection of ancient Chinese poetry. Mado's delicate, precise animal poems can also be partnered with those found in Jack Prelutsky's animal anthology, *Beauty of the Beast: Poems* (Knopf, 1997) beautifully illustrated by Meilo So. Children may also enjoy exploring other picture books by Japanese illustrator Mitsumasa Anno or delving into cut paper art or *papel picado* via Carmen Lomas Garza's book *Making Magic Windows* (Children's Book Press, 1999).

For an extra treat, try to locate a guest reader able to read and speak Japanese, if possible. For example, the poem "Sleep" (*The Animals*) has wonderful imagery comparing our eyelids to "blinds" and suggesting that all creatures lower their blinds "So as not to cause / A single dream / To be mixed / With any other." Since both the English and the Japanese versions of the poem are presented, it is possible to experiment with reading the lines as if they were written for two voices. The Japanese volunteer can read the poem in Japanese, followed by a second volunteer reading in English. Then BOTH readers read their version simultaneously, in both Japanese and English. Just be sure to encourage the readers to pause at the end of each line and start the next line together. It may take a bit of practice, but it can be quite a powerful listening and language experience. Children who speak a language other than English may want to try translating one of their favorite English poems and orchestrating a read aloud in both their languages.

The Magic Pocket: Selected Poems (McElderry, 1992) is Mado's second book of poetry available in Japanese and English and contains the same thoughtful and delicate poems about an even wider range of subjects. Lead children in comparing his style to that of Valerie Worth in her "small poem" collections. Or for an interesting twist, share the lovely *Cool Melons Turn to Frogs: The Life and Poems of Issa* by Matthew Gollub (Lee and Low, 1998), a picture books that is half biography and half haiku or Jack Prelutsky's collection of animal haiku, *If Not for the Cat* (Greenwillow, 2004), or the "urban haiku" of *Stone Bench in an Empty Park* compiled by Paul Janeczko (Orchard, 2000). Haiku is an ancient Japanese form of poetry that has been a staple of many library collections for years. Unfortunately, many readers may not realize that Japanese poets write many other forms of poetry besides haiku. Mado's poem collections help broaden those notions of Japanese poetry.

David McCord

DAVID McCORD'S POETRY

David McCord was noted for his creative, rhythmic, and often whimsical poems. He invented a new style, "symmetrics," a five-line verse form attributed to him by the *American Heritage Dictionary*. He wrote more than 500 poems and was the author or editor of more than 50 books, including a dozen collections of poetry for children:

> *Far and Few: Rhymes of the Never Was and Always Is* (Little, Brown, 1952)
>
> *Take Sky: More Rhymes of the Never Was and Always Is* (Little, Brown, 1962)
>
> *All Day Long: Fifty Rhymes of the Never Was and Always Is* (Little, Brown, 1966)

Every Time I Climb a Tree (contains selections from *Far and Few*, *Take Sky*, and *All Day Long*, Little, Brown 1967)

For Me to Say: Rhymes of the Never Was and Always Is (Little, Brown, 1970)

Mr. Bidery's Spidery Garden (Harrap, 1972)

Pen, Paper and Poem (Rinehart, 1973)

Away and Ago: Rhymes of the Never Was and Always Is (Little, Brown, 1975)

The Star in the Pail (Little, Brown, 1975)

One at a Time: His Collected Poems for the Young (Little, Brown, 1980)

Speak Up: More Rhymes of the Never Was and Always Is (Little, Brown, 1980)

All Small (Little, Brown, 1986)

Many of McCord's most popular poems are gathered in *Every Time I Climb a Tree*, such as, "Every Time I Climb a Tree," "This Is My Rock," as well as "The Pickety Fence" and "Bananas and Cream." Children will continue to find pleasure in McCord's use of sound, syncopation, wordplay, and wonder. And Simont's colorful paintings perfectly extend, but don't overwhelm the 25 poems in this collection. Many of these poems also lend themselves to choral reading and child participation. For example in the poems, "Every Time I Climb a Tree" and "This is My Rock" the title lines serve as a repeated refrain for children to chant throughout the poem when it is read aloud. The poem "Bananas and Cream" includes seven stanzas that are ideal for group read aloud with a different small group for each stanza, and a repeated stanza for the whole group to chant throughout. And of course one must try a sample of bananas and cream after reading the poem.

Look for David McCord's classic poem, "Books Fall Open" (*All Day Long*) to share during National Children's Book Week or any other book celebration. It expresses the joy of reading and could be combined with J. Patrick Lewis' poem, "Read...Think...Dream" (from *The Bookworm's Feast: A Potluck of Poems*, Dial 1999) or Joyce Sidman's poem "This Book" available on her Web site (http://www.joycesidman.com/bookmark.html) and as a lovely downloadable bookmark.

David McCord's enormous legacy was acknowledged by Mary Ann Hoberman in her poem "Take Sound" (in Paul Janeczko's *Seeing the Blue Between*, Candlewick, 2002), composed in honor of her receiving the NCTE Poetry Award. She acknowledged that she was echoing the title and cadence of his poem, "Take Sky." It focuses on the pleasures of sharing the sounds and words of poetry with children and is a great way to begin a poetry lesson or unit.

Eve Merriam

EVE MERRIAM'S POETRY

Eve Merriam's prolific body of writing comprises a wide variety of works including poetry, plays, and nonfiction for adults, approximately 40 picture books and nonfiction titles for children, as well as over 20 poetry books and anthologies. Her poetry is characterized as smart, playful, and lively and often explores the sounds and origins of words. In her later works, she tackled social issues and topics of racism, sexism, and environmental concerns. A partial listing of her poetry for children includes:

There Is No Rhyme for Silver (Atheneum, 1962)

It Doesn't Always Have to Rhyme (Atheneum, 1964)

Catch a Little Rhyme (Atheneum, 1966)

Finding a Poem (Atheneum, 1970)

Out Loud (Atheneum, 1973)

Rainbow Writing (Atheneum, 1976)

A Word or Two with You: New Rhymes for Young Readers (Atheneum, 1981)

If Only I Could Tell You: Poetry for Young Lovers and Dreamers (Knopf, 1983)

Jamboree: Rhymes for All Times (Dell, 1984)

A Sky Full of Poems (Dell, 1986)

Fresh Paint: New Poems (Macmillan, 1986)

A Poem for a Pickle: Funnybone Verses (Morrow, 1989)

Chortles: New and Selected Wordplay Poems (Morrow, 1989)

The Singing Green: New and Selected Poems for All Seasons (HarperCollins, 1992)

Higgle Wiggle: Happy Rhymes (Morrow, 1994)

Blackberry Ink: Poems (HarperCollins, 1994)

You Be Good and I'll Be Night: Jump on the Bed Poems (Turtleback, 1994)

Halloween ABC, re-released as *Spooky ABC* (Simon & Schuster, 2002)

Check out *The Singing Green* for a sampling of several of Merriam's poems from previous out-of-print collections, including "The Poem as a Door," one of several poems Merriam has penned that try to describe what poems are and how poets create poetry. Look for other Merriam poems about poetry such as "Where is a Poem?" from *There is No Rhyme for Silver*, "How to Eat a Poem" from *A Sky Full of Poems*, and "'I,' Says the Poem" from *A Sky Full of Poems*. These gems are often included in general poetry anthologies and are wonderful examples to introduce a poetry lesson or label the poetry book area.

Blackberry Ink is another wonderful Merriam collection popular for its humor and nonsense. For example, the poem, "Five Little Monsters" is a favorite of many children and is a natural for reading aloud and pantomiming. There is a line of dialogue for five children (as five "monsters") holding a bowl and a wooden spoon for stirring. Follow up with more humorous monster poems by Douglas Florian (*Monster Motel*, Harcourt, 1993) or Marilyn Singer (*Creature Carnival*, Hyperion, 2004).

For younger readers, seek out Merriam's *You Be Good and I'll Be Night: Jump on the Bed Poems* (Turtleback, 1994) with poems for sharing together out loud. For example, one counting rhyme invites children to countdown together as the train leaves the station in the poem. Link these rhymes with Mary Ann Hoberman's charming collection, *The Llama Who Had No Pajama: 100 Favorite Poems* (Harcourt, 1998). These are poem treats for children to take home and share with their families.

The poem, "Reach for a Book," was written by Eve Merriam especially for the annual bookmark produced for National Children's Book Week sponsored by the Children's Book Council (CBC) every November. Many of these bookmark poems including Merriam's were gathered in one poetry collection, *Book Poems: Poems from National Children's Book Week, 1959–1998*, edited by Mary Perrotta Rich (Children's Book Council, 1998). Merriam's poem celebrates the many reasons that readers choose books and uses clever wordplay and word coining to express this. Each of the five stanzas of the poem begins with the line "reach for a book"—an ideal refrain for the children to perform while a narrator reads the remaining lines. In repeated readings, add gestures and facial expressions to convey "reaching," "dancing," etc. Consider recruiting someone with knowledge of American Sign Language (ASL) to translate the poem into sign and learn it along with the children.

Lilian Moore

LILIAN MOORE'S POETRY

Lilian Moore has authored over 30 picture books for children, many with animal characters or about topics of daily life familiar to very young children. Several of these were even adapted into short films. In addition, she created over a dozen works of poetry that encourage children to wonder and imagine, including:

I Feel the Same Way (Atheneum, 1967)

I Thought I Heard the City (Atheneum, 1969)

Sam's Place: Poems from the Country (Atheneum, 1973)

Spooky Rhymes and Riddles (Scholastic, 1973)

See My Lovely Poison Ivy, and Other Verses about Witches, Ghosts, and Things (Atheneum, 1975)

Think of Shadows (Atheneum, 1980)

Something New Begins (Atheneum, 1982)

Adam Mouse's Book of Poems (Atheneum, 1992)

I Never Did That Before (Atheneum, 1995)

Poems Have Roots: New Poems (Atheneum, 1997)

I'm Small, and Other Verses (Candlewick Press, 2001)

Mural on Second Avenue, and Other City Poems (Candlewick Press, 2004)

Beware, Take Care (Holt, 2006)

Moore also compiled poem anthologies such as *Go with the Poem* (McGraw-Hill, 1979) and *Sunflakes: Poems for Children* (Clarion, 1992), and collaborated with colleagues to gather *Catch Your Breath: A Book of Shivery Poems* compiled with Lawrence Webster (Garrard, 1973) and *To See the World Afresh* compiled with Judith Thurman (Atheneum, 1974).

Lilian Moore brings a child's eye view to her poetry about the trials and tribulations of struggling with the mini-milestones of growing up like tying shoelaces, finger painting, negotiating jungle bars, etc. Look for her collections, *I Never Did That Before* (Atheneum, 1995) and *I'm Small, and Other Verses* (Candlewick Press, 2001) to share poems while incorporating movement and pantomime. Combine these with other similar poetry books about childhood experiences such as Rebecca Kai Dotlich's *Lemonade Sun: And Other Summer Poems* (Boyds Mills Press, 1998), Mary Ann Hoberman's *The Llama Who Had No Pajama: 100 Favorite Poems* (Harcourt, 1998), or Alice Schertle's *Teddy Bear, Teddy Bear* (HarperCollins, 2003).

Nature and environmental themes are the focus of many of her poetry collections. For example, *Poems Have Roots* contains "A River Doesn't Have to Die" a poem about her fight to save the Hudson River, along with end notes that provide background information on the locales depicted in many of the poems. Link this collection with other nature-focused poetry books such as Aileen Fisher's *Sing of the Earth and Sky: Poems about Our Planet and the Wonders Beyond* (Boyds Mills Press, 2003), Kristine O'Connell George's *Old Elm Speaks: Tree Poems* (Clarion, 1998), Marilyn Singer's *Footprints on the Roof: Poems about the Earth* (Knopf, 2002) or Jane Yolen's *Color Me a Rhyme: Nature Poems for Young People* (Wordsong/Boyds Mills Press, 2000). To extend the learning, children can research ecological issues that touch their lives such as recycling or participate in clean-up efforts in a local park or roadside (with supervision).

Lilian Moore also covers the urban landscape in her poetry with works such as *Mural on Second Avenue and Other City Poems*, which features poems about the city park, shop windows, skylines and bridges, and construction sites. Connect this with Eloise Greenfield's *Night on Neighborhood Street* (Dial, 1991) or Carole Boston Weatherford's collection, *Sidewalk Chalk: Poems of the City* (Wordsong/Boyds Mills Press, 2001). Investigate opportunities for children to create urban art themselves such as sidewalk drawing, murals, posters, flyers, etc.

Pat Mora

http://www.patmora.com/

PAT MORA'S BIO

Pat Mora was born on January 19, 1942, in El Paso, Texas and grew up in a bilingual home. Both her maternal and paternal grandparents migrated from Mexico to El Paso to escape the revolution in the early twentieth century. Mora went on to earn both her bachelor's and master's degrees from Texas Western College, now the University of Texas at El Paso. She taught English at the secondary and college levels and briefly hosted a radio talk show. She worked as an administrator, lecturer, and activist, and gives poetry readings, workshops, and presentations around the world. She continues her efforts as a literacy advocate in promoting El Día de los Niños/El Dia de los Libros (Children's Day/Book Day) held on April 30th· a national day to celebrate children and literacy. She is married and the mother of three grown children. Her hobbies include traveling, reading, walking, and visiting friends and family.

Pat Mora's work has garnered many awards and recognitions, including a Kellogg National Fellowship, a National Endowment for the Arts Fellowship, the Cooperative Children's Book Center Choices Award, inclusion on the Americas Award Commended List, an International Reading Association Notable Books for Global Society distinction, and the Tomás Rivera Mexican American Children's Book Award, among others.

PAT MORA'S POETRY

Pat Mora has written in a variety of genres including poetry for children and adults, nonfiction, and children's picture books, including *Tomás and the Library Lady* by Pat Mora (Knopf, 1997), *Confetti: Poems for Children* (Lee & Low Books, 1996/1999), and *My Own True Name: New and Selected Poems for Young Adults* (Arte Público Press, 2000). Many of her works are written in two languages (English interwoven with Spanish words and phrases), and in bilingual editions, which is especially inviting for Spanish speaking children and also instructional for children not fluent in Spanish.

Mora has also created an anthology of poetry by other Latino/Latina poets in *Love to Mamá: A Tribute to Mothers* (Lee & Low Books, 2001). Fourteen poets write in both English and Spanish about the love, joy, and humor to be found in the bonds between mothers, grandmothers, and children. Tie this with Myra Cohn Livingston's anthology, *Poems for Mothers* (Holiday House, 1988) or Janet Wong's *The Rainbow Hand: Poems about*

Mothers and Children (Simon & Schuster, 2000), or even Javaka Steptoe's collection, *In Daddy's Arms I Am Tall: African Americans Celebrating Fathers* (Lee & Low Books, 2001). For poems about families, seek out *Fathers, Mothers, Sisters, Brothers: A Collection of Family Poems* (Little, Brown, 2001) by Mary Ann Hoberman or *Hopscotch Love: A Family Treasury of Love Poems* (Lothrop, Lee & Shepard, 1999) by Nikki Grimes. Children can choose a favorite poem to read aloud to a family member on Mother's Day, Father's Day, Grandparent's Day or a special birthday in English or Spanish.

Pat Mora reflects her own feelings and experiences growing up in the Southwest in her poems in *This Big Sky* (Scholastic, 1998). She celebrates the people, the animals, and the landscape of the region. Follow up with her pictures books, *Listen to the Desert—Oye Al Desierto* (Clarion Books, 1994) or *The Desert Is My Mother—El Desierto es Mi Madre* (Arte Público Press, 1994). For other poetry with a strong sense of place, look for Diane Siebert's poem picture books such as *Mojave* (Crowell, 1988). Children may want to try making sand art projects to accompany a favorite poem, dyeing sand, and layering it into see-through glass containers or "painting" Southwestern images on paper with glue and then sprinkling sand on the wet glue for color and texture.

For young children, Mora has authored both alphabet and counting books with rhyming text which once again naturally incorporate Spanish and English words. This includes *¡Marimba!: Animales from A to Z* (Clarion, 2006) and *Uno Dos Tres, One, Two, Three* (Clarion, 1996). Both tell engaging and even humorous stories, while also celebrating the gift of being bilingual. Pair these with *Gathering the Sun: An Alphabet in Spanish and English* by Alma FlorAda (Rayo, 2001) and *Diez Deditos: Ten Little Fingers & Other Play Rhymes and Action Songs from Latin America* by José-Luis Orozco (Penguin, 2002) for additional examples of using the letters and numbers as a frame for making a book of poems and songs.

Pat Mora's *Confetti* is available in two formats, in English with Spanish words intermingled (*Confetti*, Lee & Low Books, 1999), and entirely in Spanish (*Confeti*, Lee & Low Books, 2006). Supplement either of these with the work of other Latino poets such as Francisco Alarcón (e.g., *Poems to Dream Together/Poemas para Soñar Juntos*, Lee and Low Books, 2005) and Jorge Argueta (*Movie in My Pillow/Una Pelicula en Mi Almohada*, Children's Book Press, 2001). For older children, look for the poetry of Gary Soto (*Canto Familiar*, Harcourt, 1995), and Lori Carlson (e.g., *Red Hot Salsa*, Holt 2005). If there are Spanish speakers in the community, invite them to participate in sharing these poems aloud in both Spanish and English. There are also several collections of Spanish/English children's nursery rhymes and songs available for sharing with younger children, such as *¡Pío peep! Traditional Spanish Nursery Rhymes* by Alma Flor Ada and Isabel Campoy (HarperCollins, 2003), *Arrorró mi Niño: Latino Lullabies and Gentle Games* (Lee and Low Books, 2004) by Lulu Delacre, and *Fiestas: A Year of Latin American Songs of Celebration* by José-Luis Orozco (Dutton, 2002). These verses incorporate music and movement which invite children to participate in the poems.

Many poets writing for young people also maintain rich and lively Web sites. They offer interesting biographical information, current booklists, and ideas and strategies for connecting kids with poetry, even for promoting poetry writing. Plus, they have an appealing look that engages kids. Some even provide opportunities for interaction and communication with the poet. There are book covers, photographs, and even audiofiles. These sites help budding poets see how poets live and work. Conversely, they can also help the poetry-phobic (teacher or librarian) feel less intimidated about poetry. It seems so friendly on the Web. Pat Mora has such an exemplary Web site with many resources to support poetry sharing. Also, look for similarly outstanding Web sites for Kristine O'Connell George, Nikki Grimes, and Janet Wong.

Lillian Morrison

LILLIAN MORRISON'S POETRY

Lillian Morrison has compiled several anthologies of folk verse geared for younger readers, from autograph rhymes to favorite sayings, including these gems:

Yours Till Niagara Falls: A Book of Autograph Verses (Harper-Collins, 1990)

Best Wishes, Amen: A New Collection of Autograph Verses (HarperTrophy, 1989)

I Scream, You Scream: A Feast of Food Rhymes (August House, 1997)

Guess Again!: Riddle Poems (August House, 2006)

It Rained All Day That Night: Autograph Album Verses and Inscriptions (August House, 2003)

Children may not think of autograph rhymes and such as poetry, but a gathering of Morrison's collections will show them that they can use poetry in their daily lives in notes to friends, signing yearbooks, or logging in to online guestbooks. Morrison's *It Rained All Day That Night* shows fun rhyme examples from previous generations as well as from the latest online shorthand. Children can add to the assortment of rhyming expressions with their own new versions and create a poster or poem of these new creations. Follow up with Morrison's food rhymes from *I Scream, You Scream* which are perfect to chant as a group. Related books would include Alvin Schwartz's *And the Green Grass Grew All Around: Folk Poetry from Everyone* (HarperCollins, 1992), *Juba This and Juba That: Stories to Tell, Songs to Sing, Rhymes to Chant, Riddles to Guess, and More*, edited by Virginia A. Tashjian (Little, Brown, 1995), and Joanna Cole and Stephanie Calmenson's *Yours Till Banana Splits 201 Autograph Rhymes* (Scholastic, 1995). All of these are ideal for sharing out loud and in choral performance.

Lillian Morrison is also particularly recognized for her sports-themed poetry, such as her own original poems in *The Sidewalk Racer, and Other Poems of Sports and Motion* (Lothrop Lee & Shepard, 1977) and *The Break Dance Kids* (Morrow, 1985), as well as in the sports anthologies she compiled:

Sprints and Distances: Sports in Poetry and the Poetry in Sport (HarperCollins, 1990)

At the Crack of the Bat: Baseball Poems (Hyperion, 1992)

Slam Dunk, Basketball Poems (Hyperion, 1997)

Way to Go: Sports Poems (Boyds Mills Press, 2001)

Invite local athletes to come as guest readers and read aloud sports poems. They can talk about their own experiences playing the game or show related sports equipment. Tie the poems with the appropriate sporting season and create displays that highlight sports poems with nonfiction books that provide additional information such as how-to books and sports biographies. For related sports poetry, look for Arnold Adoff's *I Am the Running Girl* (Harper, 1979), *Sports Pages* (Lippincott, 1986), or *The Basket Counts* (Simon & Schuster, 2000) or Charles R. Smith's poem picture books, *Rimshots* (Dutton, 1999), *Short Takes: Fast-Break Basketball Poetry* (Dutton, 2001) or *Diamond Life: Baseball Sights, Sounds, and Swings* (Orchard, 2004).

Morrison also compiled an anthology of "girlpower" poetry, *More Spice Than Sugar* (Houghton Mifflin, 2001), with three sections of poems dealing with women's identity, women in sports, and women's rights, plus an appendix that includes helpful background information. Link this book with *All by Herself: 14 Girls Who Made a Difference: Poems* (Harcourt, 1999) by Ann Whitford Paul or *Vherses: A Celebration Of Outstanding Women* (Creative Editions, 2005) by J. Patrick Lewis or look for Cheryl Harness' biography collections, *Rabble Rousers: Twenty American Women Who Made a Difference* (Dutton, 2003) or *Remember the Ladies: 100 Great American Women* (HarperCollins, 2001). Once again, invite guest readers to share poems out loud, particularly women in the community who hold leadership positions.

Naomi Shihab Nye

NAOMI SHIHAB NYE'S POETRY

Naomi Nye has a gift for bringing poets from many paths together. She has compiled several distinctive anthologies that include poetry from around the world such as *This Same Sky: A Collection of Poems from Around the World* (Four Winds Press, 1992), *The Tree is Older Than You Are: A Bilingual Gathering of Poems and Stories from Mexico* (Simon & Schuster, 1995), and *The Space Between Our Footsteps: Poems and Paintings from the Middle East* (Simon & Schuster, 1998) which was adapted as *The Flag of Childhood: Poems from the Middle East* (Aladdin, 2002). Her young adult poetry anthologies are also rich and varied including, *What Have You Lost?* (Greenwillow, 1999), *Is This Forever, or What? Poems and Paintings from Texas* (Greenwillow, 2004), and *I Feel a Little Jumpy Around You: A Book of Her Poems and His Poems Collected in Pairs* (Simon & Schuster, 1996), coedited with Paul Janeczko.

Nye's own original poetry is also quite powerful, and is respectful of children's appetite for both light and serious themes, such as in *Come With Me: Poems for a Journey* (Greenwillow, 2000), *A Maze Me: Poems for Girls* (Greenwillow, 2005), and *Nineteen Varieties of the Gazelle* (Greenwillow, 2002). In addition to her poetry for children and young adults, Nye has authored picture books, novels for young adults, and poetry and essays for adults. Naomi Shihab Nye's Palestinian American heritage is often present in her work, although she more often celebrates universal human qualities, rather than differences. Her picture book, *Sitti's Secrets* (Macmillan, 1994), young adult novel, *Habibi* (Simon & Schuster, 1996), and her poetry collections, *Nineteen Varieties of the Gazelle* and *The Space Between Our Footsteps: Poems and Paintings from the Middle East* can be shared in tandem for a fascinating window into her heritage.

Many of the poems from her international and multicultural collections lend themselves to being read aloud in creative ways, giving voice to these different cultural perspectives. For example, try the poem, "Napoleon," originally by Miroslav Holub from the Czech Republic (from *This Same Sky*). This poem describes a classroom moment with perspectives of a teacher/narrator, a class as a whole, and one individual student (named "Frankie"). Read the poem out loud once and then divide the lines up for "Frankie" and for "the class." See if the children agree that classrooms around the world have many things in common. Many poems offer similar combinations of whole group, small group, individual, and other read aloud configurations. Link Nye's multicultural collections with other similar anthologies such as Belinda Rochelle's *Words with Wings: A Treasury of African American Poetry and Art* (HarperCollins, 2000), and Charles Sullivan's anthology, *Here Is My Kingdom: Hispanic-American Literature and Art for Young People* (Abrams, 1994).

With some bilingual poems, it is possible to read the two versions aloud as if they were written for two voices. For example, Jennifer Clement's poem, Arbol de Limon/ Lemon Tree" appears in both Spanish and English (translated by Consuelo de Aerenlund) in Naomi Shihab Nye's collection, *This Tree Is Older Than You Are*. If there is a Spanish speaker volunteer in the audience, she/he can read the poem in Spanish, followed by a reading in English. Then *both* readers read their version simultaneously, in both Spanish and English. Just be sure to encourage the readers to pause at the end of each line and start the next line together. The effect is very powerful.

Naomi Shihab Nye has also authored a collection of poetry that celebrates and inspires girls with *A Maze Me: Poems for Girls* (Greenwillow, 2005). Combine this with other girl-themed poetry anthologies such as: *Ferocious Girls, Steamroller Boys, and Other Poems in Between* (Orchard, 2000) by Timothy Bush, *Dreams of Glory: Poems Starring Girls* (Atheneum, 1995) compiled by Isabel Joshlin Glaser, *All by Herself: 14 Girls Who Made a Difference: Poems* (Harcourt, 1999) by Ann Whitford Paul, *Hoop Queens* (Candlewick, 2003) by Charles R. Smith, and *Heroes and She-Roes: Poems Of Amazing and Everyday Heroes* (Dial, 2005) and *Vherses: A Celebration of Outstanding Women* (Creative Editions, 2005) both by J. Patrick Lewis. For nonfiction resource books, consult Milton Meltzer's *Ten Queens: Portraits of Women of Power* (Dutton, 1998) or Kathleen Krull's *Lives of Extraordinary Women* (Harcourt, 2000).

And in the picture book poem collection, *Come With Me: Poems for a Journey*, Nye provides free verse poems that can prompt discussion. For example, the poem "Torn Map" speculates how friends might be reunited by a torn map. And of course, this poem can come to life by bringing in maps to study, discuss, and even tear and recreate as poem-art. Pair this book with Nancy Willard's collection of "journey" poems, *Step Lightly: Poems for the Journey* (Harcourt, 1998).

For a special tribute to libraries, seek out one of Nye's poems, "Because of Libraries We Can Say These Things," from her collection of poetry for adults entitled *Fuel* (BOA Editions, 1998). Link this poem with short stories about the power of books and libraries in *When I Went to the Library* edited by Debora Pearson (Groundwood, 2002) or *In the Stacks* edited by Michael Cart (Overlook, 2003). For a follow up with children look for Naomi Nye's poem "The List" from *A Maze Me: Poems For Girls* (Greenwillow, 2005), an interesting examination of how readers choose which books to read.

It can also be very meaningful to share poem collections that include works authored by children such as Naomi Shihab Nye's compilation, *Salting the Ocean: 100 Poems by Young Poets* (Greenwillow, 2000), or *Ten Second Rain Showers* (Simon & Schuster, 1996), and *Soft Hay Will Catch You: Poems by Young People* (Simon & Schuster, 2004) both edited by Sanford Lyne. These are each beautiful books full of unsentimental and authentic young voices and provide an invitation to see children as capable of poetic expression, too.

Mary O'Neill

MARY O'NEILL'S BIO

Mary O'Neill was born on February 16, 1908, in New York, and died on January 2, 1990, in Yuma, Arizona. She was married and had three children. She grew up in Berea, Ohio, and attended Cleveland College of Western Reserve University and the University of Michigan, and then worked as an advertising copywriter in Ohio before moving to New York to establish her own advertising agency with a partner. She eventually turned to freelance writing and is probably best known for her poetry collection, *Hailstones and Halibut Bones*, published in 1961, which was selected by the New York Times as one of 100 best children's books of the year.

MARY O'NEILL'S POETRY

O'Neill's poetry focuses on many teachable concepts like color, words, numbers, wind, and sounds, and uses list-like rhyming poems to communicate attributes of concepts in metaphors that children could understand. Her work includes:

Hailstones and Halibut Bones: Adventures in Color (Doubleday, 1961/1990)

People I'd Like to Keep (Doubleday, 1964)

Words, Words, Words (Doubleday, 1966)

What Is That Sound! (Atheneum, 1966)

Take a Number (Doubleday, 1968)

Winds (Doubleday, 1970)

Although most of her books are out of print, many of her poems continue to appear in anthologies. For example, her poem "Take a Number" is reprinted in Lee Bennett Hopkins' compilation, *Marvelous Math: A Book of Poems* (Simon & Schuster, 1997). Two of the poems from her book *What Is That Sound!* were published in picture book form with illustrations by Cynthia Jabar, *The Sound of Day, the Sound of Night* (Farrar, Straus & Giroux, 2003). But her best known and still accessible work is surely *Hailstones and Halibut Bones*, a handy introduction to color words and images for young children and to color similes and metaphors for older children. In this collection of 12 color poems, O'Neill offers a poetic exploration of the tangible and intangible ways we might view purple, gold, black, brown, blue, gray, white, orange, red, pink, green, and yellow. For each poem's title she poses the question, "What is . . . ?" and answers it with list-like rhyming poems that include objects of the designated color, but go on to suggest sounds, tastes, smells, and feelings also evoked by the color. Illustrated with color montages by Leonard Weisgard in 1961 and later reissued with Wallner's illustrations, *Hailstones* offers children a template for the ways that poems can portray images and sensory experiences.

O'Neill's "color" poems also lend themselves to choral reading with children because of their linear format. For example, with the poem, "What is Black?" by Mary O'Neill, which expresses images of things that are black in color or feeling, each line can be read by a different volunteer for an easy group reading. And with a bit of extra preparation, the lines of the poem can be combined based on the phrasing of the poem, since some lines work best in pairs. For example these two lines, "The sound of black is/ 'Boom! Boom! Boom!'" can be read by two readers, but the next two lines, "Echoing in/ An empty room" seem to go together naturally for one voice to read aloud. To follow up, try to gather some of the objects mentioned in the poem, such as charcoal, licorice, patent leather shoes to accompany the poem reading. Seek out other poetry books about color, such as Jane Yolen's *Color Me a Rhyme: Nature Poems for Young People* (Wordsong/Boyds Mills Press, 2000) and Pat Mora's *Confetti: Poems for Children* (Lee & Low Books, 1996). Older children may enjoy creating a slide show for the poem, hunting for images for each line or two of the poem and presenting it as an audio-visual poem read aloud experience. For younger readers, match this book with Margaret Wise Brown's classic picture book *The Important Book* (HarperTrophy, 1990), which also looks at other associations for common objects.

Mary O'Neill provides a similar litany of associations for SOUNDS in her two poems reprinted in the book, *The Sound of Day, the Sound of Night*. Here, however, the illustrations provide a story thread that suggests what might be happening behind the poems. The language is full of descriptions of sounds such as buses honking, bells ringing, tiptoeing on stairs, and kittens purring that children can attempt to provide as a background soundtrack during repeated read alouds. Follow up with a picture book about another family's busy morning, *Buzz* by Janet Wong (Harcourt, 2000). Older children may enjoy taking other of O'Neill's poems and creating their own illustrated versions of the lines of the poem to share with younger children.

José-Luis Orozco

http://www.joseluisorozco.com/

JOSÉ-LUIS OROZCO'S BIO

José-Luis Orozco was born in Mexico City, where he performed with the Mexico City Boys Choir. He traveled extensively as an adult, exploring at least 32 countries. He settled in California where he earned his bachelor's degree from the University of California at Berkeley, and his master's degree from the University of San Francisco. Orozco is also known as a singer and performer, as well as a poet and translator, and participated in the National Book Festival in Washington, DC. He lives in Los Angeles, California, where he has four children and two grandchildren.

JOSÉ-LUIS OROZCO'S POETRY

With young children, sharing songs in picture book form may help them see the poetry around them in the familiar tunes and lyrics they have grown up with. The cultural traditions of each community are rich with examples of songs strong with rhyme and rhythm in nearly every language. José-Luis Orozco's work is an outstanding example of this. He has selected, arranged, and translated several lively collections of songs and rhymes from Spanish-speaking countries, including *De Colores and Other Latin-American Folk Songs for Children* (Dutton, 1994), *Diez Deditos: Ten Little Fingers and Other Play Rhymes and Action Songs from Latin America* (Dutton, 1997), and *Fiestas: A Year of Latin American Songs of Celebration* (Dutton, 2002), each joyfully illustrated by Elisa Kleven.

Orozco introduces folksongs in both English and Spanish in his book *De Colores*, with both lyrics and music provided for each song. Partner this book with the illustrated collections by Lulu Delacre's *Arrorró Mi Niño: Latino Lullabies and Gentle Games* (Lee & Low Books, 2004), *Arroz con Leche: Popular Songs and Rhymes from Latin America* (Scholastic, 1989) and *Las Navidades: Popular Christmas Songs from Latin America* (Scholastic, 1992). For songs from other cultural traditions, seek out *All Night, All Day: A Child's First Book of African-American Spirituals* collected and beautifully illustrated by Ashley Bryan (1991), Chinese traditional rhymes such as Mingfong Ho's *Maples in the Mist: Children's Poems from the Tang Dynasty* (Lothrop, 1996), or the comprehensive resource of American folksongs in Amy Cohn's *From Sea to Shining Sea: A Treasury of American*

Folklore and Folk Songs (1993). Invite children to write down and illustrate their own songs and lullabies from their families, neighborhoods, or cultural traditions.

In *Diez Deditos*, Oroszco presents 34 bilingual (English/Spanish) selections from Spanish-speaking countries including diagrams illustrating finger, hand, and/or body movements appropriate to each rhyme or song. Brief explanatory notes precede each piece and often capture Orozco's intensely personal recollections of his own childhood. Fingerplays and rhymes with motions and movement are a staple of early introductions to poetry for many children. Combine Orozco's book with *¡Pío Peep! Traditional Spanish Nursery Rhymes* by Alma Flor Ada and Isabel Campoy (HarperCollins, 2003) or the bilingual collection, *Grandmother's Nursery Rhymes/Las Nanas de Abuelita: Lullabies, Tongue Twisters, and Riddles from South America/Canciones de Cuna, Trabalenguas y Adivinanzas de Suramerica* by Nelly Palacio Jaramillo (Holt, 1994). If you are a Spanish speaker or work with Spanish-speaking children, reading these poems aloud in both the Spanish and the English can be very inviting and celebrate both language and culture at the same time.

For additional collections of action rhymes, look for *Head, Shoulders, Knees, and Toes and Other Action Rhymes* by Zita Newcome (Candlewick, 2000), *Wiggle Waggle Fun: Stories and Rhymes for the Very Very Young* by Margaret Mayo (Knopf, 2002), and Michael Foreman's *Playtime Rhymes* (Candlewick, 2002). Jane Yolen provides two helpful international collections of children's rhymes: *Street Rhymes from Around the World* (Boyds Mills Press, 2000) and *Sleep Rhymes Around the World* (Boyds Mills/Wordsong, 1994). For slightly older children, consult Alvin Schwartz's collection *And the Green Grass Grew All Around: Folk Poetry from Everyone* (HarperCollins, 1992), *Juba This and Juba That: Stories to Tell, Songs to Sing, Rhymes to Chant, Riddles to Guess, and More*, edited by Virginia A. Tashjian (Little, Brown, 1995), Judy Sierra's *Schoolyard Rhymes: Kids' Own Rhymes for Rope Skipping, Hand Clapping, Ball Bouncing, and Just Plain Fun* (Knopf, 2005), or Stephanie Calmenson and Joanna Cole's collections such as *Miss Mary Mack* (Morrow, 1990). For children who missed Mother Goose in their preschool years, are new to nursery rhymes in English versions, or simply want to revisit them for the pleasure of the sounds and rhythms (and the memories of young childhood), these resources are well worth revisiting again and again.

José-Luis Orozco has gathered songs for special occasions in his anthology, *Fiestas: A Year of Latin American Songs of Celebration*. Extend this work with *A Treasury of Children's Songs: Forty Favorites to Sing and Play* collected by Dan Fox (Holt, 2003), books of patriotic songs such as *O Beautiful for Spacious Skies* by Katharine Lee Bates (Chronicle, 1994) or summer camp songs in *Camp Granada: Sing-Along Camp Songs* selected and illustrated by Frane Lessac (Holt, 2003). For older children, studying song lyrics can be a "back door" approach to inviting readers into the world of poetry. Writing down lyrics for favorite songs (or finding them on CD liners or the Web) can help young people look closely at the use of language, word choice, phrasing, use of repetition, and figurative language in a poetic format that they might find more relevant.

Jack Prelutsky

http://www.jackprelutsky.com

JACK PRELUTSKY'S POETRY

Jack Prelutsky is a prolific writer, with many collections of poetry to his credit, including enormously popular anthologies he has compiled of other poets' works, such as *The Random House Book of Poetry for Children* (Random House, 1983), *Read-Aloud Rhymes for the Very Young* (Knopf, 1986), *The Beauty of the Beast* (Knopf, 1997), and *The 20th Century Children's Poetry Treasury* (Knopf, 1999). In addition, there are many collections of his own popular poetry available including books organized around topics such as *Tyrannosaurus Was a Beast: Dinosaur Poems* (Mulberry, 1993) and *The Dragons are Singing Tonight* (HarperTrophy, 1998). His holiday poems are also very appealing: *It's Halloween* (HarperTrophy, 1996), *It's Christmas* (HarperTrophy, 1995), *It's Thanksgiving* (HarperTrophy, 1996), and *It's Valentine's Day* (HarperTrophy, 1996), and are also available in one single audio anthology from HarperChildrensAudio (2005). For younger children, he created a kind of "American Mother Goose" with nursery rhymes that reference cities and places in the United States, rather than European sites such as "London Bridge" or "Banbury Cross" in his collections, *Ride a Purple Pelican* (Greenwillow, 1986) and *Beneath a Blue Umbrella* (Greenwillow, 1990). Match these with Canadian poet Dennis Lee's rhymes in *Dinosaur Dinner with a Slice of Alligator Pie* (Random House, 1997) edited by Prelutsky.

Jack Prelutsky became established as a poetic dynamo with the publication of *The New Kid on the Block* (Greenwillow, 1984), his best-selling collection of 100+ poems illustrated by cartoonist James Stevenson with understated comic genius on every page. With poems that are nearly childhood standards now, like "Homework! Oh, Homework!" and "Bleezer's Ice Cream," the music of Prelutsky's verse is irresistible. Since the publication of *New Kid*, he rivals Shel Silverstein for name recognition in the field of children's poetry. Equally popular companion books followed, including *Something Big Has Been Here* (Greenwillow, 1990), *A Pizza the Size of the Sun* (Greenwillow, 1996), and *It's Raining Pigs & Noodles* (Greenwillow, 2000). A fifth installment is slated for publication in 2008: *My Dog May Be a Genius* (Greenwillow, 2008).

Many of Prelutsky's poems lend themselves to choral reading and poem performance in a variety of ways. For example, his poems with repeated lines or refrains provide a natural opportunity for group participation on the refrain. One of the most popular examples for this is "Homework, Oh, Homework" (from *The New Kid on the Block*) by Jack Prelutsky. This popular lament on the woes of homework touches a responsive chord among children. Combine this poem with other school poetry collected by Carol Diggory Shields. Another Prelutsky poem very effective with this strategy is "Louder than a Clap of Thunder!" (from *The New Kid on the Block*) with the repetition of the word "louder" which describes the narrator's father's snoring. The word "louder" begins many, but not all of the lines of the poem, so alert the children to that variation ahead of time as their voices get louder and louder. One other possibility for spontaneous group participation is to find poems that use counting numbers or days of the week as part of the poem. For example, Prelutsky's poem, "Countdown" (from *It's Halloween*), begins "There are ten ghosts in the pantry" and the children can shout out on the counting words, beginning with "TEN." Use cut-out paper ghosts to act out the actions of the poem.

Once children are familiar with poems that are read aloud in parts, try dividing the group in half to read poems in a call and response method. This works well for Prelutsky's Thanksgiving poem, "I'm Thankful" (from *The New Kid on the Block*) which juxtaposes two alternating points of view on thankfulness line by line. And for line-around readings, try "Bleezer's Ice Cream" (from *The New Kid on the Block)* with individual or pairs of children each taking one of the crazy ice cream flavor lines. Pair this with Shel Silvertsein's "Eighteen Flavors" from *Where the Sidewalk Ends* (Harper & Row, 1974/2004). To follow up, make two-dimensional paper ice cream cones and pile them high with multicolored scoops named in new wacky flavors by the children themselves.

Reading poems in a canon is one other strategy that involves timing and overlapping lines and can be challenging for children. But when you find a suitable poem and try this technique with children, you will find it is fun and challenging, just like singing "Row, row, row, your boat" in a canon. Try "I'm Much Too Tired to Play Tonight" (from *Something BIG Has Been Here*). Physically clapping the rhythm of the poem together can also help with reading a poem canon-style.

Another strategy for performing Prelutsky's poetry is singing. Count the beats in the first line or two of the poem; then count the beats in the first line or two of the song to see if they match. Many of Jack Prelutsky's poems, in particular, match song tunes, which may not be surprising when one remembers he was a singer and musician before turning to poetry. Try his poem "Allosaurus" (from *Tyrannosaurus was a Beast: Dinosaur Poems*), a poem describing the ferocious qualities of this dinosaur sung to the tune of "Row, Row, Row Your Boat." It's a hilarious juxtaposition of lyrics and tune. Challenge the children to match other of his dinosaur poems to song tunes. Look for more poems to sing in Alan Katz's books such as *Take Me Out of the Bathtub and Other Silly Dilly Songs* (McElderry, 2001).

Jack Prelutsky has also published poetry in other forms, for example, his collection of animal haiku is illustrated by Ted Rand in *If Not for the Cat* (Greenwillow, 2004). For a completely different approach suitable for older children, look for the "urban haiku" of *Stone Bench in an Empty Park* (Orchard, 2000). And seek out Prelutsky's *Poems of A. Nonny Mouse* (Knopf, 1989) and *A. Nonny Mouse Writes Again! Poems* (Knopf, 1993) for poems by "Anonymous." Children can create characters, like cutout paper mice, and display them with their own favorite poems by "Anonymous" or "A. Nonny Mouse."

Alice Schertle

ALICE SCHERTLE'S BIO

Alice Schertle (rhymes with "turtle") was born on April 7, 1941, in Los Angeles, California. She earned her bachelor's degree from the University of Southern California and taught elementary school in Inglewood, California. She married and had three children and began writing for young people as her children were growing up. Her first collection of poetry, *How Now, Brown Cow*, was published in 1994. Later, she moved from California to New Salem, Massachusetts, to experience another climate. Her work has won many awards including Parents' Choice citations, the Christopher Award, *School Library Journal* Best Book, and American Library Association Notable Book.

ALICE SCHERTLE'S POETRY

Alice Schertle has created an impressive body of work including over two dozen picture books, often told in rhyme, as well as the "Cathy and Company" picture book series for young children, and poetry collections known for their graceful use of language and often tongue-in-cheek sense of humor. She writes about animals, memories, childhood, and about the writing process itself. Schertle also provides masterful examples of many different forms of poetry from nursery rhymes to free verse, from haiku to parodies.

In her first poetry book, *How Now, Brown Cow?* (Browndeer, 1994), Schertle created a clever collection of 15 poems capturing the "cow's-eye" view of the world, many with a wry sense of humor. She plays with the words "cow" and "moo" in the poems, and with familiar phrases such as "the grass is greener" "til the cows come home," and "driving" the cows to great effect. The poem, "Taradiddle" takes the nursery rhyme, "Hey, Diddle Diddle" to the next hilarious level. For a fun connection to this single poem, look for Mini Grey's book, *The Adventures of the Dish and the Spoon* (Knopf, 2006). To extend this witty look at cow life, share *Click, Clack, Moo: Cows That Type* by Doreen Cronin (Simon & Schuster, 2000). Children who are familiar with cows may want to imagine additional adventures that cows could have and create poems and pictures to express them. Or another, more familiar animal could serve as the subject for an exploration of the hidden thoughts, feelings, and adventures of animals.

Alice Schertle has also created a poetry book for cat lovers with *I Am the Cat* (Lothrop, Lee & Shepard, 1999). This collection alternates narrative poems with haiku in describing different qualities of cats and kittens. Combine this with Jack Prelutsky's haiku collection, *If Not for the Cat* (Greenwillow,

2004) or contrast the cat perspective with the dog lover's point of view in Kristine O'Connell George's *Little Dog Poems* (Clarion, 1999) and it's sequel, *Little Dog and Duncan* (Clarion, 2002), or the dual perspectives in Jane Yolen's *Raining Cats and Dogs* (Harcourt, 1993), or Douglas Florian's *Bow Wow Meow Meow; It's Rhyming Cats and Dogs* (Harcourt, 2003). Stage a mock debate comparing dogs and cats as preferred pets, with children using these poems as examples of their pet's best qualities. Children may also enjoy voting for the "cutest" kitten or puppy on the Web sites: http://puppywar.com/ or http://kittenwar.com/.

Schertle turns her attention to interesting, exotic, and endangered animals in her poem collection, *Advice for a Frog and Other Poems* (Lothrop, Lee & Shepard, 1995). Through 14 poems full of wordplay and vivid description, she introduces the harpy eagle, the frilled lizard, the black rhino, and more. Pair this with Jane Yolen's poems about ancient animal breeds in *The Originals* (Philomel, 1998). For additional factual information, consult alphabet books featuring extinct or endangered animals such as Jerry Pallotta's *The Extinct Alphabet Book* (Charlesbridge, 1993), Sandra and William Markle's *Gone Forever: An Alphabet of Extinct Animals* (Atheneum, 1998) or Ann Jonas's *Aardvarks, Disembark* (Puffin, 1994). Children can investigate organizations that are dedicated to protecting animals and endangered species such as the Wildlife Conservation Society. They can write letters for more information or explore relevant Web sites such as http://www.kidsgowild.com.

Younger children may enjoy Schertle's poem collection, *Teddy Bear, Teddy Bear* (HarperCollins, 2003) with charming rhymes that describe the lives of much loved teddy bears. Invite children to bring their favorite teddy bear or other stuffed animal to hug while teddy bear poems are shared out loud. Follow up with other teddy bear rhymes such as the "Jesse Bear" books by Nancy White Carlstrom or the classic "Teddy bear, teddy bear, turn around" rhyme or "The teddy bears picnic" song.

Alice Schertle also adapted English versions of Spanish rhymes for young children in *¡Pío Peep! Traditional Spanish Nursery Rhymes* by Alma Flor Ada and F. Isabel Campoy (HarperCollins, 2003). If there are Spanish speakers in the community, invite them to participate in sharing these poems aloud in both Spanish and English. For additional rhymes in Spanish/English and in other languages, look for José-Luis Orozco's *Diez Deditos: Ten Little Fingers and Other Play Rhymes and Action Songs from Latin America* (Dutton, 1997) or Jane Yolen's *Street Rhymes from Around the World* (Boyds Mills Press, 2000).

Schertle's poetry book, *Keepers* (Lothrop, 1996) features poems on a motley collection of objects and moments that conjure up special feelings and memories, from a special key to a walk in the woods. Look for objects, photographs, or props to show when sharing poems from this collection. Place them in a decorated "treasure" box for extra effect. Link with Janet Wong's *Knock on Wood: Poems about Superstitions* (Simon & Schuster, 2003) or

Kristine O'Connell George's *Fold Me a Poem* (Harcourt, 2005) to conjure up more memories or create new treasures.

A Lucky Thing (Harcourt 1999) is Alice Schertle's examination of the writing process itself from a young girl's point of view as she observes the world around her. Combine this book with Nikki Grimes' works about writing: *Jazmin's Notebook* (Dial, 1998) and *A Dime a Dozen* (Dial, 1998), or Eloise Greenfield's poem anthology about books, words, and language, *In the Land of Words* (HarperCollins, 2004). Make simple, homemade notebooks with children and encourage them to keep their own journals of thoughts and poems.

Carol Diggory Shields

CAROL DIGGORY SHIELDS' BIO

Carol Diggory Shields was born December 1, 1945, grew up in Glen Head, New York, and attended Juniata College in Pennsylvania, where she earned a bachelor's degree in English. Later, she earned a master's degree in therapeutic recreation from San Francisco State University and worked with children in hospitals and group homes. She was also a stuffed toy designer before becoming a children's librarian. She is married, has three children, and currently resides in Prunedale, California.

CAROL DIGGORY SHIELDS' POETRY

Shields has authored picture books for young children as well as poetry collections which excel at channeling the child point of view. Look for her perspective on kids and classrooms in her poem collection: *Lunch Money and Other Poems about School* (Dutton, 1995) and its sequel, *Almost Late to School: And More School Poems* (Dutton, 2005). She has also created the curriculum-friendly "BrainJuice" collections: *BrainJuice: Science, Fresh Squeezed!* (Handprint, 2003), *BrainJuice: English, Fresh Squeezed!* (Handprint, 2004), and *BrainJuice: American History, Fresh Squeezed* (Handprint, 2005). Each of these is known for her distinctive humor and creative use of various poem formats.

The school poems in *Lunch Money*, for example, lend themselves to child participation because of their strong rhythms and fun subject matter. For example, the poem "Code" must be read aloud as if one has a stuffy nose and cannot pronounce "cold" correctly. Have tissues handy as a prop. Or the poem "Outside/Inside" repeats the words "outside" and "inside" as the poem contrasts the world outside the window with the world inside the classroom. Hold up a sign with "inside" on one side and "outside" on the other to cue children when to join in with the correct word.

Once children are familiar with poems read aloud in parts, they can be divided into two groups to read poems in a "call and response" method. The best poems for this poetry performance strategy are those whose lines are structured in a kind of back and forth way. "Clock-watching" by Carol Diggory Shields (*Lunch Money*, 1995) is a wonderful example with one group narrating and an alternating group intoning, "Click, jump, Click, jump" as everyone waits for time to slowly pass.

Using multiple small groups is another approach in bringing poems to life with oral presentation. In "And the Answer Is..." by Carol Diggory Shields there are two major stanzas, one reflecting the point of view of a student who is anxious that the teacher might call on him/her, the other the perspective of a student who is eager to be called on to give the answer. In general, a different group reads a different stanza. Ask for volunteers, or invite children to participate as they are clustered in their seats. One other quick and effective method is to use a deck of cards, give each child a card, and use red/black (2 groups) or suits of cards (4 groups) to designate group identity.

Some poems are list-like in their structure and these work well for what is sometimes called line-around choral reading in which individual voices read individual lines. Try "Pledge" by Carol Diggory Shields with individual voices alternating with the whole class in this mock recitation of the Pledge of Allegiance. [Be sure to clarify what the correct Pledge of Allegiance should sound like beforehand.] The poem "Oral Report" (from *Almost Late)* is also ideal for ten volunteers to read the worries the narrator has about delivering an oral report in front of the class.

Probably the most difficult form of choral reading is reading aloud poetry for two voices. This requires synchronization of reading as well as getting used to two completely different lines sometimes being read at the same time. Shields offers just such a poem, "Poem for Two Voices" reflecting the special bond between two friends (in *Almost Late).* Children can choose their favorite Carol D. Shields' "school" poem to prepare for an oral reading (with a friend or group) at an Open House, PTA/PTO meeting, or for an open mike reading.

Shields' poetry can also be linked with other poems about teachers, children, and school to contrast poetic styles. For example, her poem "After School" (in *Almost Late)* wonders what happens in a classroom *after* everyone leaves and can be shared alongside Gary Soto's poem "What Fernie Thought" *Fearless Fernie: Hanging Out with Fernie & Me* (Putnam, 2002) which describes a child's surprise at encountering the teacher at the grocery store and not "living" in the classroom. Other humorous poetry collections that focus specifically on school include: Kalli Dakos' *If You're Not Here, Please Raise Your Hand* (Four Winds Press, 1990) and *Don't Read This Book, Whatever You Do*! (Four Winds Press, 1993), David Harrison's *Somebody Catch my Homework* (Boyds Mills Press, 1993), *I Thought I'd Take My Rat to School* (Little, Brown, 1993) by Dorothy and X. J. Kennedy, or for older children, *The Dog Ate My Homework* by Sara Holbrook (Boyds Mills Press, 1997).

Carol Diggory Shields' "BrainJuice" collections of science, English, and history-related poetry can be combined with other subject-specific poetry anthologies by Lee Bennett Hopkins such as *Marvelous Math* (Simon & Schuster, 1997), *Spectacular Science: A Book of Poems* (Simon & Schuster, 1999), *Wonderful Words: Poems About Reading, Writing, Speaking, and Listening* (Simon & Schuster, 2004), and *Hand in Hand: An American History through Poetry* (Simon & Schuster, 1994). Children can choose their favorite poem to share with teachers of those subject areas as a fun poetry break.

Joyce Sidman

http://www.joycesidman.com

JOYCE SIDMAN'S BIO

Joyce Sidman was born on born June 4, 1956, in Hartford, Connecticut. She is the middle sister of three, and spent summers at a camp in Maine. From an early age, she felt motivated to write, and started writing as far back as elementary school. She discovered poetry in high school, encouraged by a sympathetic teacher. She earned her bachelor's degree in German from Wesleyan University in Connecticut, and a teaching certificate at Macalester College in Minnesota. Joyce lives in Wayzata, Minnesota, with her husband and two sons, near the edge of a large woodland. When she isn't writing, she enjoys teaching via weeklong poetry-writing residences in the schools. Her hobbies include gardening, identifying birds, insects and frogs, reading, and baking cookies. Her poetry has already garnered several awards including designation as Junior Library Guild selections, *Horn Book* Fanfare book, *Voice of Youth Advocates* Poetry Pick, Bulletin Blue Ribbon Book, as well as the Lee Bennett Hopkins Poetry Award for *Song of the Water Boatman and Other Pond Poems*.

JOYCE SIDMAN'S POETRY

Much of Joyce Sidman's poetry centers on the subject of the natural world and is marked by poetic innovation and an elegance of expression. Often she weaves together scientific information alongside poetic descriptions. One such example is her collection, *Just Us Two: Poems About Animal Dads* (Millbrook, 2000). Sidman offers 11 poems that depict the special relationship between a father and his young, be they wolves, frogs, or penguins. The poems include accurate information as well as an emotional hook and are colorfully illustrated with cut paper collages. Connect this with nonfiction picture books such as *Animal Dads* (Houghton Mifflin, 1997) by Sneed B. Collard III, illustrated by Steve Jenkins or with more poetry via *Animal Poems* (Farrar, Straus & Giroux, 2007) by Valerie Worth also illustrated by Steve Jenkins. Make the leap to human fathers with Javaka Steptoe's anthology, *In Daddy's Arms I Am Tall: African Americans Celebrating Fathers* (Lee & Low, 1997) or Mary Ann Hoberman's poems in *Fathers, Mothers, Sisters, Brothers: A Collection of Family Poems* (Little, Brown, 1991). Children can choose their favorite "dad" poem and tape record it and illustrate it as a gift for a father, grandfather or other special man in their lives.

Sidman has two other nature-themed collections that are somewhat parallel in form and layout: *Song of the Water Boatman: Pond Poems* illustrated by Beckie Prange (Houghton Mifflin, 2005) and *Butterfly Eyes and Other Secrets of the Meadow* illustrated by Beth Krommes (Houghton Mifflin, 2006). In *Song of the Water Boatman*, we learn about the diverse life of ponds through eleven poems in various forms, including haiku, free verse, and cumulative rhymes. Each poem is accompanied by a prose paragraph with further scientific information. A glossary of science terms makes it even more useful for instruction. Pair this with *Hey There, Stinkbug!* by Leslie Bulion (Charlesbridge, 2006), another collection that combines poems with paragraphs of scientific information. Sidman's *Butterfly Eyes* focuses on the ecosystem of the meadow with poems posed as riddles, followed by narrative explanations. Once again a helpful glossary is provided. For appropriate companion books seek out Marilyn Singer's *Turtle in July* (Macmillan, 1989) and *Fireflies at Midnight* (Atheneum, 2003). All together, these collections introduce us to creatures of the insect world through descriptive poems and beautiful illustrations. Bring a bug in a jar (with air holes) for children to study and describe. They can create thumbprint insect characters or draw pictures to accompany their writing. If the local natural history museum has guest speakers available, invite them to visit and bring insect specimens to show.

For a completely different collection, look for Joyce Sidman's book, *Eureka! Poems About Inventors* (Millbrook, 2002), with 16 poems describing a range of people who have created something new through imagination, investigation, and pure persistence, with subjects such as scientist Marie Curie and the inventor of the Frisbee. Link these poems with the fascinating profiles of incidental inventions in Charlotte Foltz Jones' *Mistakes That Worked* (Doubleday, 1994) and *Accidents May Happen* (Delacorte, 1998) or Judith St. George's humorous nonfiction book, *So You Want to Be An Inventor?* (Puffin, 2005). Look for J. Patrick Lewis' poems about famous accomplishments in *A Burst of Firsts* (Dial, 2001) for another connection.

Check out Joyce Sidman's Web site for in-depth guides full of activities for using her books with children. She provides information, photographs, links, and even printable resources like a lovely bookmark with an original poem about books to share.

Diane Siebert

DIANE SIEBERT'S POETRY

Diane Siebert may be best known for her poem picture books which take a single poem and spread the lines of the poem across the pages of a picture book. Some of these tell stories and some are more reflective descriptions, but all are beautifully illustrated by a variety of well-known artists. These works can be approached as picture books for sharing, as poems for reading aloud, or as visual introductions to a place or concept. Several work together in a complementary fashion, combining her poetry books around a transportation theme or a focus on the landscape of the United States.

Truck Song (Crowell, 1984), *Train Song* (Crowell, 1990), *Plane Song* (HarperCollins, 1993), *Motorcycle Song* (HarperCollins, 2002) are four of Siebert's "song" poems that describe various modes of transportation. Sharing them with children shows kids that poems can be about all kinds of things, including trucks, trains, planes, and motorcycles. In addition, nonfiction books can complement these poetry selections by providing additional information in contrasting styles. For example, look for nonfiction picture books such as Gail Gibbons' *Trucks* (Trophy, 1985) and *Fill It Up!* (HarperCollins, 1985) or Paul Collicutt's *This Train* (Farrar, Straus & Giroux, 2001), *This Plane* (Farrar, Straus & Giroux, 2002), and *This Truck* (Farrar, Straus & Giroux, 2004). Or pair the poem book with a related work of fiction, such as *Train Song* with Angela Johnson's picture book, *I Dream of Trains* (Simon & Schuster, 2003) or *Motorcycle Song* with the short novel by Beverly Cleary, *The Mouse and the Motorcycle* (reissued HarperCollins, 2006). In addition, Siebert's poetry lends itself to being read aloud, strong with the rhythms of the journey in each "song." Children can echo each line as it is read aloud or pipe in on alternating lines. And of course, many lines call for motions or movement, too.

Diane Siebert has also authored a set of poem picture books that celebrate special places in the topography of the United States including *Heartland* (Crowell, 1989), *Mojave* (Crowell, 1988), *Sierra* (HarperCollins, 1991), *Mississippi* (HarperCollins, 2001), and *Cave* (HarperCollins, 2000). Each is beautifully illustrated and describes natural phenomenon with both information and grace. Any one of the books can serve as a springboard for further study of farming, deserts, mountains, rivers, and caves. Seek out additional poetry collections that center on the American landscape such as Marilyn Singer's *Monday on the Mississippi* (Holt, 2005), Frank Asch's *Sawgrass Poems: A View of the Everglades* (Harcourt, 1996), or Joseph Bruchac's *The Earth Under Sky Bear's Feet: Native American Poems of the Land* (Philomel, 1995). And of course, nonfiction books can be consulted for further information about these various sites and landmarks, including series books, almanacs, and travel guides. Children who are planning road trips can choose a favorite poem and take it along to read as a theme poem for their journey or as a break on a picnic or just to share outside. Or for a special poetry program, assemble a slide show of scenes and images of one of these locales (mountains, desserts, farmland, etc.) to accompany an oral reading of any of the corresponding Siebert poems.

Continue this focus on the land with Siebert's poetry book, *Rhyolite: The True Story of a Ghost Town* (Clarion Books, 2003). Here she tells the story of the rise and fall of a Nevada gold-mining town through rhyme and poetry. Contrast this with examples of other poet's tributes to the land and its history, such as *I Have Heard of a Land* by Joyce Carol Thomas (HarperTrophy, 2000), Pat Mora's *This Big Sky* (Scholastic, 1998), or *Is It Far to Zanzibar?* by Nikki Grimes (HarperCollins, 2000).

Diane Siebert's poetry collection, *Tour America: A Journey through Poems and Art* (Chronicle Books, 2006) is a longer work with individual poem tributes to states, sites, and structures across the United States, each accompanied by an illustration, a map, and an explanatory paragraph. Here, any of the poems can stand on its own, as a kind of read-aloud tour of the United States. Younger children may enjoy pairing this book with Peter Sis' *Train of States* (Greenwillow, 2004). Or match Siebert's collection with other geography-themed poetry collections, such as *A World of Wonders: Geographic Travels in Verse and Rhyme* (Dial Books, 2002), *Monumental Verses* (National Geographic, 2005) by J. Patrick Lewis, or Lee Bennett Hopkins' anthology *Got Geography!* (Greenwillow, 2006). Locate the sites for children's favorite poems on a map and encourage them to find or create poems for places on the map that are not yet in the poetry books.

Shel Silverstein

http://www.shelsilverstein.com/indexSite.html

SHEL SILVERSTEIN'S BIO

One of America's most successful children's poets ever, Shel Silverstein was born in Chicago, Illinois, on September 25, 1930, and died in 1999. He began his career as an artist drawing cartoons for the military newspaper *Stars and Stripes* during the 1950s and went on to write songs, lyrics, and plays as well as act in movies.

In 1963, Silverstein reluctantly began his career as a children's book author and illustrator encouraged by Harper editor Ursula Nordstrom with his first book, *Lafcadio, the Lion Who Shot Back*. The following year he gained even greater success with *The Giving Tree* (HarperCollins). But it was his poetry collections that put him on the map. In 1974, Silverstein published his first collection of poems, *Where the Sidewalk Ends*, which became an instant hit. His next poetry collection, *A Light in the Attic*, sold over half a million copies in the first year. His third collection, *Falling Up*, was equally successful.

SHEL SILVERSTEIN'S POETRY

Surveys of children's preferences as well as bookselling statistics confirm kids of all ages respond strongly to the poetry of Shel Silverstein. He wrote about everyday events and childhood experiences, often with an outrageous sense of the absurd. His pen and ink cartoon illustrations add another layer of originality and appeal. His three major collections of poetry, *Where the Sidewalk Ends* (Harper & Row, 1974/2004), *A Light in the Attic* (Harper & Row, 1981) and *Falling Up* (HarperCollins, 1996), are also available as audio recordings narrated in Silverstein's own gravelly voice. Listening to the poems read by the poet himself is a very special experience and the audio versions are worth acquiring.

Children enjoy browsing through Silverstein's poetry anthologies and spontaneously sharing their favorite poems. With his strong rhyme and rhythm and outrageous sense of fun, his work lends itself to being read aloud, too. In addition, his distinctive pen and ink sketches capture children's imaginations, and it's difficult to imagine his anthologies without those illustrations. Children may enjoy trying their own hand at cartooning. Refer to Lee Ames' helpful "how to" drawing guides such as *Draw 50 Famous Cartoons: The Step-by-Step Way to Draw Your Favorite Cartoon Characters* (Broadway, 1985). Children may also enjoy the pen and ink sketches and oddball humor of Douglas Florian's *Bing Bang Boing* (Harcourt, 1994), or

Judith Viorst's *If I Were in Charge of the World* (Atheneum, 1981), or the wickedly clever poetry of John Ciardi and X. J. Kennedy.

Many of the individual poems in Silverstein's anthologies are now very familiar to children and lend themselves to a variety of activities. For example, Silverstein's "Boa Constrictor" poem begs for movement wiggling the body parts gradually "eaten" by the boa. Or pair the poem, "Sarah Cynthia Sylvia Stout" with Ogden Nash's classic "The Tale of Custard the Dragon." In Shel Silverstein's poem "Smart," each stanza reveals a bit more about a child's misunderstanding about the value of a dollar bill and various coins. Use this poem to look at the values of American bills and coins, especially for children who are new to the United States. Many of Silverstein's poems are list-like in their structure and these work well for what is sometimes called "linearound" choral reading in which individual voices read individual lines. However, be sure the poem is familiar before students volunteer for individual lines. Always begin by reading the poem aloud to them. For example, children might try "What if?" by Shel Silverstein (*A Light In the Attic*) with each "what-if worry" read by a different voice. Even more activities and audioclips are available on the fun and engaging Web site that Silverstein's publisher maintains at http://www.shelsilverstein.com.

Marilyn Singer

http://www.marilynsinger.net

MARILYN SINGER'S BIO

Marilyn Singer was born on October 3, 1948, in New York and grew up and went to college there, too. She started out as a high school English teacher but soon moved to writing full time. While visiting the Brooklyn Botanic Garden one day, she began to write about insect characters that she had created when she was eight years old. With her husband's encouragement, she joined a writer's critique group and soon published her first book, *The Dog Who Insisted He Wasn't* (Dutton, 1976). Now a prolific author of more than 75 children's books, Singer has created poetry, fairly tales, picture books, novels, mysteries, and nonfiction on a variety of topics. Her work has been recognized as an IRA Children's Choice book, ALA Best Book for Young Adults, NCTE Notable Trade Book in Language Arts, Reading Rainbow selection, *New York Times* Best Children's Book, *School Library Journal* Best Book, etc.

Singer enjoys animals, nature, hiking, the theater, independent and avant-garde films, tap dancing, singing, Japanese flower arranging, meditation, gardening, and computer adventure games. Her diverse and far-ranging interests are often reflected in the rich variety of her writing.

MARILYN SINGER'S POETRY

From her first book about a beloved subject, dogs, Marilyn Singer has created many works on a wide variety of topics that children enjoy. In fact, pairing her poetry with her nonfiction on a similar topic can be an interesting way to show children how one writer can try different writing styles. Share the poems from *It's Hard to Read a Map with a Beagle on Your Lap* (Holt, 1993) alongside the informative *A Dog's Gotta Do What a Dog's Gotta Do: Dogs at Work* (Holt, 2000), or *How to Talk to Your Dog* (HarperTrophy, 2003) by Jean Craighead George.

Nature is the dominant theme in her poetry collections, *Turtle in July* (Macmillan, 1989) and *Fireflies at Midnight* (Atheneum, 2003). In these two parallel works, Singer mimics the rhythms and sounds of the animals she portrays. Each poem begs to be read aloud, perhaps with simple motions or a costume cap portraying the frog, the robin, the turtle, etc.

Marilyn Singer has authored three other poetry collections that make a powerful environmental set. Each is a lovely narrow size (9×5) illustrated with elegant minimalist India ink paintings on rice paper by Meilo So.

* *Footprints on the Roof: Poems about the Earth* (Knopf, 2002)
* *How to Cross a Pond: Poems about Water* (Knopf, 2003)
* *Central Heating: Poems about Fire and Warmth* (Knopf, 2005)

These free verse poems are gems of description and imagery and may inspire young writers to look for the elements of earth, water, and fire that surround them in their everyday lives. Partner this set with Joan Bransfield Graham's books of concrete poetry, *Splish Splash* (Houghton Mifflin, 2001) and *Flicker Flash* (Houghton Mifflin, 2003) to inspire children to create their own visual representations of earth, water, or fire.

For humor and nonsense, seek out Singer's poetry books, *Creature Carnival* (Hyperion, 2004) and its companion book, *Monster Museum* (Hyperion, 2001). Children may be surprised to find that poems can be about Godzilla, vampires, Bigfoot, and other creepy characters. Accompanied by gleefully gruesome cartoon illustrations by Gus Grimly, these fun poems are full of wordplay and absurdity. Don't be surprised if these collections inspire imitations. Have a set of Halloween "monster" masks handy for children to wear during the "creature feature" read aloud. Conclude with poems from Douglas Florian's *Monster Motel* (Harcourt, 1993).

Family is the focus for two other Marilyn Singer collections, *In My Tent* (Macmillan, 1992) and *Family Reunion* (Atheneum, 1994). These poems about family campouts and reunions show children that even common everyday life experiences can also be the subject of poetry. They can also be fun for reading aloud during family programs and events. Pair them with Kristine O'Connell George's collection, *Toasting Marshmallows: Camping Poems* (Clarion, 2001) or Nikki Grimes' *Hopscotch Love: A Family Treasury of Love Poems* (Lothrop, Lee & Shepard, 1999). Plan a poetry picnic for sharing these and other family poems outside spread out on a tablecloth or under a big tent.

Because Singer is so prolific, it is possible to pair many of her works (poem book and poem book, poetry with nonfiction, poetry and fiction) for added impact. Children can see how an author's ideas spill over beyond a single book and in many different directions. Whether reading her "geography" poems in *Monday on the Mississippi* (Holt, 2005) or her poems from the perspectives of two young girls, *All We Needed to Say: Poems about School from Tanya and Sophie* (Atheneum, 1996), an in-depth study of one featured poet can be helpful for aspiring young writers. Simply through examining Marilyn Singer's body of work, children can begin to see how a poet's thinking takes shape.

Charles R. Smith, Jr.

http://www.charlesrsmithjr.com/

CHARLES R. SMITH JR.'S BIO

Charles R. Smith Jr. grew up in Compton, California, and loved books and basketball in nearly equal measure. In high school he was exposed to photography during a yearbook class and was "hooked." He enrolled at the Brooks Institute of Photography in Santa Barbara, California, and when he graduated headed to New York City to work as a professional photographer. Eventually, he showed his portfolio to a children's book art director, and his first book, *Rimshots*, emerged. More photo-illustrated books have followed, as well as a music CD, "Charles R. Smith, Jr., Portrait of a Poet." After the birth of his first child he moved to Poughkeepsie, New York, where he currently resides.

CHARLES R. SMITH JR.'S POETRY

Charles R. Smith Jr. is known for his creative photo collages as well as for his high-energy writing style in both his picture books and his poetry. His basketball-themed poetry collections, in particular, are very popular with middle-grade readers—boys and girls. His first book, *Rimshots* (Dutton, 1999), is a collection of poems and story vignettes, an in-your-face urban experience of basketball playing. The sepia-toned photographs throughout the book capture faceless players in active poses playing pick-up games on outdoor courts. Many of the poems are concrete, using the expansive white space to spread the poem out in a visual representation of the action, such as "Fastbreak" and "The Sweetest Roll." Other "list" poems such as "Excuses, Excuses," and "Everything I Need to Know in Life, I Learned from Basketball" beg for student involvement in choral readings or in writing extensions. Follow up with his parallel collection of basketball poetry entitled, *Short Takes: Fast-Break Basketball Poetry* (Dutton, 2001) which captures moments of play and uses blurred photographs to great effect. Combine these with Arnold Adoff's poetry collection, *The Basket Counts* (Simon & Schuster, 2000). Adoff's use of free verse, concrete poetry, and word play portrays everything from a game of pickup basketball to the playing of wheelchair athletes. Also, look for Lillian Morrison's sports poetry anthology, *Slam Dunk, Basketball Poems* (Turtleback Books, 1995) with odes to Magic Johnson, Michael Jordan, and more. Invite students to share their own experiences of the ball, the court, and the moves they know best.

Two other Smith poetry collections make a natural pairing: *Hoop Kings* (Candlewick, 2004) and *Hoop Queens* (Candlewick, 2003). Each is an extra tall picture book filled with poems that celebrate some of the top basketball players in the game—both men and women. This time, however, Smith has focused on the poetry and utilizes images captured by official sports photographers. Look for related nonfiction books such as *Hoops with Swoopes* by Susan Kuklin and Sheryl Swoopes, full of action verbs and short phrases spread out among photographs of WNBA star Sheryl Swoopes playing basketball (Hyperion, 2001) or sports biographies such as Joan Anderson's *Rookie—Tamika Whitmore's First Year in the WNBA* (Dutton, 2000). Children can research more current information on favorite players on the Internet or via sports magazines.

Switch to baseball and share Smith's poem collection, *Diamond Life: Baseball Sights, Sounds, and Swings* (Orchard, 2004) full of shape or concrete poems in an innovative layout, using multiple fonts and enhanced photographs. The increased number of sports poetry currently available is refreshing and offers great potential for active participation in the oral sharing of verse. Children can act out the motions suggested by the words for poetry performance or be encouraged to explore their own extracurricular interests (sports, hobbies, interests) as they write about their experiences and share their worlds. They can work together to create a sports poetry display complete with poetry books, poet info, sporting equipment, and memorabilia.

Charles R. Smith Jr. has also created a music-based collection of poems, entitled *Perfect Harmony: A Musical Journey with the Boys Choir of Harlem* (Jump at the Sun, 2002). Here he introduces music theory and choral music basics in rhythmic poems that suggest a rap tempo. Inspired by the Boys Choir of Harlem, he proclaims, "It all begins / with the power/of one," but when combined, the voices of Harlem "roar!" Look for audio recordings of the Choir to share with children. Follow up with Bryan Collier's picture book, *Uptown* (Holt, 2000), illustrated in distinctive collages that invite the reader to take a tour of Harlem, noting both the personal and historic markers that make it a special place. The text for each scene begins with "Uptown is . . .," with details reflecting one child's point of view. For older readers, seek out Walter Dean Myers' poetry book with many perspectives, *Here in Harlem: Poems in Many Voices* (Holiday House, 2004). Invite children to draw or write about their own neighborhoods or communities.

For more ideas, activities, and even audio downloads of several poems from his books, check out Charles R. Smith's Web site. He has information, photographs, links, and more for children, teachers, and librarians in a very appealing format.

Gary Soto

http://www.garysoto.com/

GARY SOTO'S BIO

Gary Soto was born on April 12, 1952, in Fresno, California. He received his bachelor's degree in English from Fresno State College in California and his Master of Fine Arts degree from the University of California at Irvine. It wasn't until he was in college that he discovered poetry and started writing. He has since published many works of poetry for both adults and children and also worked as Associate Professor of Chicano Studies and English at the University of California at Berkeley. He is married and has a daughter, Mariko, who works as a veterinarian.

GARY SOTO'S POETRY

Dip into Gary Soto's poetry with the poem, "Ode to My Library" from *Neighborhood Odes* (Harcourt, 1992) which is almost a short story it shares so many details about a small town library. Its description of the physical space of the library mentions the rooms, the books, the globe, the maps, the fish tank, the pencil sharpener, etc. Talk with children about what details of the library children might note in a poem they might compose. For an artistic follow up, children might enjoy creating an illustration of the library described or even a comic strip sequence illustrating the many scenes suggested in the poem: dropping a globe in the library, the librarian reading, a child studying about the Incas, the three birds "talking," the phonograph and the headphones, and the fantasy sequences of the imagined airplane trip, the remembered summer read-a-thon, and the mural painting. Older students may also enjoy "Ode to Family Photographs," a celebration of cock-eyed family pictures taken with a crooked camera. Invite children to bring their own crazy photographs to share, along with the stories behind them.

Another wonderful collection of Soto's poetry is *Canto Familiar* (Harcourt, 1995) which includes 25 poems dealing with experiences of Mexican American children growing up in the United States. These poems are written with lively voices that beg to be read aloud. Many of the poems deal with themes common to all children. A perennial favorite is "My Teacher in the Market Place" which describes a child's surprise at encountering her teacher at the grocery store and not "living" in the classroom. Soto returns to this subject in another poem, "What Fernie Thought" in *Fearless Fernie: Hanging Out with Fernie & Me* (Putnam, 2002). The poem "Spanish" is a great example for celebrating the value of being bilingual. Look to Monica Gunning's *America, My New Home* (Boyds Mills Press, 2004) or Janet Wong's *Good Luck Gold* (Simon & Schuster, 1994) for additional perspectives on language and culture.

Gary Soto's collection, *A Fire in My Hands* (Harcourt, 1996), includes rich, descriptive poems as well as the short author insights that are offered at the beginning of each poem, so helpful to budding poets. In this new reissue, there are also 10 new poems (with a paragraph on where the idea for each of these poems came from, too), as well as an author's note by Soto at the end. Like Pat Mora (*My Own True Name: New and Selected Poems for Young Adults*, Arte Público Press, 2000), Soto conveys many details about growing up Mexican American, but this time in California. He also uses a handful of Spanish words here and there in his poems. The context provides meaning, and the words provide flavor. For other parallel voices, look for poetry by Nikki Grimes, Ron Koertge, and Kathi Appelt.

For middle-school students, Soto has created a set of poems woven together to tell a story about a friendship between two boys, *Fearless Fernie: Hanging Out with Fernie & Me* (Putnam, 2002) and a sequel, *Worlds Apart: Fernie and Me* (Putnam, 2005), with his usual blend of humor and humiliation. Match this with similar poem-story collections such as *Relatively Speaking: Poems about Family* (Orchard, 1999) from the point of view of a younger brother or *Girl Coming in for a Landing* (Knopf, 2002) by April Halprin Wayland, a girl's perspective. For more poetry about middle-school woes, look for Kristine O'Connell George's *Swimming Upstream: Middle School Poems* (Clarion, 2002) and *A Maze Me: Poems for Girls* by Naomi Shihab Nye (Greenwillow, 2005). Kids can choose their favorite poems to send to a friend via text messaging.

Gary Soto's memoir *Living Up the Street* (Laurel Leaf, 1992) received an American Book Award and shares many vignettes based on his life, as does the essay collection, *A Summer Life* (Laurel Leaf, 1991). He is also well known for his engaging picture books such as *Chato's Kitchen* (Putnam, 1995) and its "Chato" sequels and the Christmas story, *Too Many Tamales* (Putnam, 1993), as well as middle-grade novels and short stories including his ground-breaking *Baseball in April* (Harcourt, 1990) and the appealing *The Skirt* (Yearling, 1994), as well as for his contemporary young adult novels, such as *Taking Sides* (Harcourt, 1991) and *The Afterlife* (Harcourt, 2003). He has also produced the film "The Pool Party" based on his short novel for young adults, as well as written the libretto for an opera entitled "Nerdlandia" and a play for young people called "Novio Boy."

Joyce Carol Thomas

http://www.joycecarolthomas.com

JOYCE CAROL THOMAS' BIO

Joyce Carol Thomas was born on May 25, 1938, in Ponca City, Oklahoma. She attended San Francisco City College and the University of San Francisco, but received her bachelor's degree from San Jose State College in California. She also earned a master's degree from Stanford University. She has worked as a telephone operator, a teacher of French and Spanish, a reading program director, and as a professor of English. Thomas has won numerous awards including Best Book and Notable citations from the American Library Association, National Council of Teachers of English, and the National Council for the Social Studies; as well as the National Book Award for Children's Fiction, the Coretta Scott King Award, and the Oklahoma Sequoyan Young Adult Book Award. She was married and has four children.

JOYCE CAROL THOMAS' POETRY

Joyce Carol Thomas has penned noteworthy poetry and plays for adults, fiction for young adults, as well as poetry collections for children that capture and celebrate African American culture in ways that help all readers acknowledge their roots. Two favorites are *Brown Honey in Broomwheat Tea* (HarperCollins, 1993) and *Gingerbread Days* (HarperCollins, 1995), both beautifully illustrated by Floyd Cooper. She has also authored picture books, board books, and retellings of folktales collected by Zora Neale Hurston. Her lyrical language and focus on family, identity, and culture is distinctive and engaging.

Joyce Thomas' free verse poems in *Brown Honey in Broomwheat Tea* (HarperTrophy, 1996) and the companion volume *Gingerbread Days* (HarperTrophy, 1997) share glimpses of family love while celebrating the beauty and heritage of all African Americans. Share the thoughtful poem, "Becoming the Tea" (from *Brown Honey in Broomwheat Tea*) and brew a cup of tea (preferably from tea leaves) to bring the poem to life. Bring gingerbread to accompany the January poem from *Gingerbread Days*, a collection of a dozen poems loosely linked to the months of the year. Pair this with Lilian Moore's poetry collection based on the calendar year, *Mural On Second Avenue and Other City Poems* (Candlewick, 2004) or Eloise Greenfield's *Night on Neighborhood Street* (Dial, 1991), a glimpse of life in an urban community, or Nikki Grimes' *Hopscotch Love: A Family Treasury of Love Poems* (Lothrop, Lee & Shepard, 1999), a heartwarming collage of family moments.

In the poems in *Crowning Glory* (HarperCollins, 2002), Thomas honors the African American traditions of braids, cornrows, dreadlocks, ribbons, and scarves in adorning the head and hair. She particularly pays tribute to women, much like Nikki Giovanni's poem, "Mattie Lou at Twelve" (*Spin a Soft Black Song*, Farrar, Straus & Giroux, 1987) or Jacqueline Woodson's picture book *Show Way* (Putnam, 2005). Follow up with Kathryn Lasky's picture book biography, *Vision of Beauty: The Story of Sarah Breedlove Walker* illustrated by Nneka Bennett (Candlewick, 2003), the founder of the Madame C.J. Walker Manufacturing Company of hair care products for black women and the richest African American woman of her time.

Thomas narrows her focus to mothers and daughters with her poetry book, *A Mother's Heart, A Daughter's Love: Poems for Us to Share* (Harper-Collins, 2001), full of poems designed to be read alone, together in a duet, or as a call and response. Connect these poems with Janet Wong's collection, *The Rainbow Hand: Poems About Mothers and Children* (Simon & Schuster, 2000) or Pat Mora's anthology, *Love to Mama: A Celebration of Mothers* (Lee and Low, 2001). Children can choose their favorite poems and tape themselves reading them to share as a special "Mother's Day" or birthday poem tribute.

For younger children, Joyce Thomas has compiled the pleasing collection, *Hush Songs: African American Lullabies* (Hyperion, 2000), featuring ten songs including lyrics, music, and introductions. This is a lovely way for parents to introduce African American lullabies to their children. Connect this book with Ashley Bryan's *All Night, All Day: A Child's First Book of African-American Spirituals* by Ashley Bryan (Aladdin, 2003) or *Let it Shine: Three Favorite Spirituals* (Atheneum, 2007). For examples of lullaby songs and poems from other cultures, seek out *Arrorró Mi Niño: Latino Lullabies and Gentle Games* (Lee & Low, 2004) or *On the Road of Stars: Native American Night Poems and Sleep Charms* (Macmillan, 1994) collected by John Bierhorst. Parents and children can work together to write down their own family bedtime songs and rhymes which the children can illustrate as a keepsake.

Judith Viorst

JUDITH VIORST'S BIO

Judith Viorst was born on February 2, 1931, in Newark, New Jersey, and earned her bachelor's degree in history from Rutgers University. She is also a graduate of the Washington Psychoanalytic Institute. She worked as a secretary and as an editor before turning to writing. She has since published collections of poetry for both children and adults, as well as picture books and nonfiction for young readers. She resides in Washington, DC, with her husband Milton, a political writer. They have three sons, Anthony, Nicholas, and Alexander. Probably her most famous children's book is *Alexander and the Terrible, Horrible, No Good, Very Bad Day*, which was first published in 1972, and has since sold over two million copies and been made into a musical as well.

JUDITH VIORST'S POETRY

Although Judith Viorst is not known primarily as a poet, her two major collections of poetry for children consistently rank at the top of children's favorites: *If I Were in Charge of the World and Other Worries: Poems for Children and Their Parents* (Aladdin, 1984) and *Sad Underwear and Other Complications: More Poems for Children and Their Parents* (Aladdin, 2000). She tackles many poignant and hilarious moments of childhood, often with "list" poems that don't rhyme—a form that many are surprised that children enjoy.

One way to make poetry come alive for children is to share poems with props and several of Viorst's poems are perfect for this approach. When we have an object to show or share that corresponds with the poem, it can make the poem more concrete for kids. They can see it, touch it, and experience a piece of the poem more directly. Try Judith Viorst's poem "Mother Doesn't Want a Dog" (from *If I Were in Charge of the World*) and pull out a rubber snake at the reading of the concluding line. Poet Janet Wong uses a similar approach with her "poetry suitcase" (http://www.janetwong.com). She has gathered an assortment of objects and realia that connect with some of her poems (e.g., a toy turtle, play telephone). She asks children to choose an object, and then shares the poem that "corresponds" with that object and explains the connection. She encourages children to do the same—choose favorite poems, find related objects, and use them as props when sharing the poem. For kids who are still kinesthetic learners, sharing props means "touching" the poem.

Many of Viorst's poems reflect the voice of a child and are ideal for inviting children to participate in choral reading and poetry performance. There are many poems for children that incorporate a linear format that lends itself to line-around reading. This includes Viorst's "It's a Wonderful World, But They Made a Few Mistakes" (from *Sad Underwear*) which begins and ends with the titular line, but has many, varied individual lines ideal for solo voices. Children can create their own list poems itemizing their wishes for changing the world. As we bring drama into poetry, we can allow children to exercise their natural wiggliness in "acting out" poems or by choosing poems with a strong point of view for role-playing. For example, Judith Viorst's poem "Credit" (from *Sad Underwear*) is a short poem about a child's frustration about an unidentified "it." The child actor can improvise what "it" might be. Combine this with Shel Silverstein's poems which are also perfect for acting out, such as "The Meehoo with an Exactlywatt" from *A Light in the Attic* (Harper, 1981).

Another strategy for sharing Viorst's poetry is through singing. This can require extra preparation, but it is irresistibly fun, matching poems to song tunes that contain the same meter in their first lines. For example, use the tune for "Row, Row, Row Your Boat" to accompany Viorst's poem, "Someday Someone Will Bet That You Can't Name All Fifty States" which leaves one state off the list. See if the children can guess which state is missing. Consult a map of the United States to locate the states and challenge children to identify them without the states labeled.

Reading poems in a canon is one other strategy that involves timing and overlapping lines and can be challenging for children. In addition, not many poems lend themselves to reading in a round since they must have a very regular beat or meter and some repetition. But with a suitable poem, it can be fun and challenging, just like singing "Row, row, row, your boat" in a canon. Try "No" by Judith Viorst (from *If I Were in Charge of the World*). Challenge children to write a counterpoem emphasizing the word "yes."

Judith Viorst's poems can also be paired with longer works of fiction that echo her humorous style. For example, "I Love Love Love My Brand-New Baby Sister" (from *Sad Underwear*) pairs nicely with Judy Blume's now classic novel, *Superfudge* (Puffin, 2003). Or link her poems, "And After a Hundred Years had Passed, Sleeping Beauty Awoke (At Last!) From Her Slumber" (and several others from *Sad Underwear*) or " ... And Then the Prince Knelt Down and Tried to Put the Glass Slipper on Cinderella's Foot" (from *If I Were in Charge of the World*) with any humorous picture book version of each of these folktales, such as *Cinder-Elly* by Frances Minter (Puffin, 1997) or *Sleeping Ugly* by Jane Yolen (Putnam, 1997). And for more hilarious rhyming versions of classic folktales, look for *Roald Dahl's Revolting Rhymes* (Knopf, 2002).

Carole Boston Weatherford

http://www.caroleweatherford.com/

CAROLE BOSTON WEATHERFORD'S BIO

Carole Boston Weatherford was born on February 13, 1936, grew up in Baltimore, Maryland, and wrote her first poem when she was in the first grade. Her father, a high school printing teacher, printed some of her early poems on index cards. Weatherford holds a Master of Fine Arts degree in creative writing from the University of North Carolina, Greensboro, and another master's degree in publications design from the University of Baltimore. Weatherford taught at Salem College, High Point University, and Guilford Technical Community College. She conducts workshops and residencies and regularly publishes a newspaper column, essays, and articles. Her hobbies include traveling, visiting museums and parks, cycling, swimming, sewing, jazz music, and gourmet food. Weatherford lives in High Point, North Carolina, with her husband and two children.

CAROLE BOSTON WEATHERFORD'S POETRY

Carole Boston Weatherford has authored poetry for children and adults, picture books, and nonfiction generally focused on aspects of African American history and culture. Her writing has been recognized with many awards and recognitions including citations on the following notable lists: International Reading Association Teachers' Choices list, National Council of Teachers of English Notables, National Council of Social Studies Notable Children's Trade Book, Carter G. Woodson Award, and Voices of Youth Advocates Poetry Picks, among others.

Weatherford captures details of daily life in her poetry collection, *Sidewalk Chalk; Poems of the City* (Wordsong/Boyds Mills Press, 2001), with poems about the laundromat, local diner, city market, barbershop, and other routine stops in a city child's life. One poem, "Sidewalk Chalk" is a rhythmic, rhyming poem describing a variety of outdoor games children enjoy. A natural extension would be to follow the poem's "directions" to draw on the sidewalk with chalk or try tic-tac-toe or other games described in the poem. For more information, look for Mary Lankford's *Hopscotch Around the World* (HarperTrophy, 1996) or share the rhymes collected by Jane Yolen in *Street Rhymes Around the World* (Shen's Books, 2000). For more "neighborhood" poetry books, seek out Eloise Greenfield's *Night on Neighborhood Street* (Dial, 1991) showing children attending church and playing games with their families or Lilian Moore's *Mural on Second Avenue and Other City Poems* (Candlewick, 2005) which features poems about the city park, shop windows, skylines and bridges, and construction sites. Children can create poem-maps of their own neighborhoods, drawing pictures of favorite places and describing them in list-like poems.

Weatherford weaves together African American history, family stories, and vanishing traditions into poems with a strong voice that invite read aloud or dramatic presentation. One outstanding example is *Remember the Bridge: Poems of a People* (Philomel, 2002) beautifully illustrated with historic photographs and art. Poem by poem, an engaging overview of African American history unfolds like a mini-museum ideal for presenting in dramatic reading. Many famous and ordinary individuals are introduced in words and images, from the slave storyteller to Harriet Tubman, the sharecropping farmer to Martin Luther King, Jr. To extend the experience, match a character poem with a picture book or biography about that individual such as Doreen Rappaport's *Martin's Big Words: The Life of Dr. Martin Luther King, Jr.* (Hyperion/Jump at the Sun, 2001) or Weatherford's own *Moses: When Harriet Tubman Led Her People to Freedom* (Hyperion/Jump at the Sun, 2006).

Carole Weatherford has created an inspiring poem picture book in *Dear Mr. Rosenwald* (Scholastic, 2006), based on the true story of how Rosenwald schools were built through donations from Julius Rosenwald, President of Sears, to rural African American communities in the South in the 1920s. Every two pages include an expressionistic illustration by R. Gregory Christie in the style of Harlem Renaissance artist, William Johnson with a first-person poem providing a snippet of the story of how one community raised the matching funds, obtained the land and supplies, and built the school themselves. Children may be inspired to research more about the Rosenwald Schools Initiative dedicated to finding and preserving these historic schools. For another poem picture book that presents a true story through poems, look for Lee Bennett Hopkins' autobiographical *Been to Yesterdays: Poems of a Life* (Wordsong/Boyds Mills Press, 1995) or older readers may enjoy reading historical novels in verse such as Helen Frost's book *The Braid* (Farrar, Straus & Giroux, 2006), the intertwining tale of two sisters surviving hardships as Scottish refugees/immigrants in the 1850s.

Carole Boston Weatherford also maintains an excellent Web site with many resources designed for educators and librarians who share poetry with children. She has lesson plans, bookmarks to print, a radio interview and other downloadable audio, study guides, a slide show, and more.

Nancy Willard

NANCY WILLARD'S POETRY

Nancy Willard has authored notable poetry, short stories, and essays for adults, as well as many rhyming picture books, poetry collections for children, and retellings of classic fairy tales such as *Beauty and the Beast.* Known for her lyrical language and use of the themes of imagination and magic, her work has been recognized with many awards including the Newbery Medal, the Lewis Carroll Shelf Award, American Book Award nomination, *New York Times* Notable book, among others.

Nancy Willard's book, *A Visit to William Blake's Inn: Poems for Innocent and Experienced Travelers*, illustrated by Alice Provensen and Martin Provensen (Harcourt, 1981) is a perfect example of her distinctive style, mixing the magical and the mundane, dreams and reality. William Blake's poetry is the inspiration for her poems in this book, and he also appears as an integral part of the poems as the innkeeper of imagination. Older readers may enjoy reading William Blake's original "Songs of Innocence and Experience" poetry. They could choose a favorite poem, like "The Tyger" and reinterpret it through illustration or imitation. Follow up with Willard's tribute to another classic poet, Robert Louis Stevenson, in *The Voyage of the Ludgate Hill: A Journey with Robert Louis Stevenson*, also illustrated by Alice Provensen and Martin Provensen (Harcourt, 1987). This humorous narrative is based on letters Stevenson wrote about his voyage from London to New York on a cargo steamer and lends itself to being read aloud. Again, this can provide a connection to the poetry of Stevenson such as *A Child's Garden of Verses* or to his novels for older readers such as *Treasure Island*. For children who want to know more about Stevenson's travels in the United States, look for Jim

Murphy's nonfiction book, *Across America on an Emigrant Train* (Clarion, 1993).

For more mystical blendings of history and nonsense, look for Willard's book, *Pish, Posh, Said Hieronymous Bosch*, illustrated by Leo and Diane Dillon (Harcourt, 1991). This poetic tribute to the fifteenth century Dutch artist Hieronymus Bosch is a playful poem about the artist's imagined housekeeper and how she copes with his "two-headed dragons" and "flying fish." Willard coins unusual words and odd phrases to great effect, much like Dr. Seuss, and kids can compare her creations such as "pickle-winged fish" to his "oobleck" and "sneetches" or to the crazy creatures of Calef Brown like the "allicatter gatorpillar" from *Flamingos on the Roof* (Houghton Mifflin, 2006). Older children may also be interested in looking at some of Bosch's original art full of inventive fantasy and bizarre nightmares.

In *The Ballad of Biddy Early*, illustrated by Barry Moser (Knopf, 1989) Willard uses poems, songs, limericks, and ballads to celebrate the memory of a nineteenth century Irish peasant woman known for her gift of healing. Both humans and animals share their perspectives on the woman and her gift of magic and mystery, witchcraft and enchantment, through 15 poems in varying styles which lend themselves to dramatic read aloud for older readers. For a different twist, pair this with the mystical poems of Juan Felipe Herrera in his bilingual collection of poetry, *Laughing Out Loud, I Fly: Poems In English In Spanish* (HarperCollins, 1998).

Younger readers will enjoy Willard's approach to the alphabet book with *An Alphabet of Angels* (Scholastic, 1994) which she illustrated herself with photographs of angel figurines and statues with accompanying rhyming captions. Look for its companion book, *The Good-Night Blessing Book* (Scholastic, 1996). Children can gather their own photographs for a homemade alphabet book and try for rhyming labels, or assemble their own collection of objects and create a "good night" book centered around those favorite items.

Nancy Willard has also gathered an anthology of poetry by other writers that she gleaned from her own favorite poems that she kept for years in a shoebox. This collection, *Step Lightly: Poems for the Journey* (Harcourt, 1998) includes a wide range of poets from Shakespeare to Neruda, from the serious to the nonsensical. Partner this anthology with another collection of "journey" poems by Naomi Shihab Nye, *Come with Me: Poems for a Journey* (Greenwillow, 2000). Encourage children to keep their own "shoebox" collection of favorite poems to read and revisit throughout their "journeys" and invite them to share which poems are their favorites and why.

Janet S. Wong

http://www.janetwong.com

JANET WONG'S BIO

Janet S. Wong was born on September 30, 1962, and grew up in California, the child of Korean and Chinese immigrants. She graduated from UCLA with a bachelor's degree in history and then obtained her law degree from Yale. However, she was not happy practicing law and decided to make a change, focusing on writing for young people instead. She has since authored nearly two dozen picture books and poetry collections. Her poems have been featured in some unusual venues, including a car-talk radio show, on 5,000 subway and bus posters as part of the New York City Metropolitan Transit Authority's "Poetry in Motion" program, and on the "Oprah" television show. She and her books have received numerous awards and honors, such as the International Reading Association's "Celebrate Literacy Award" for exemplary service in the promotion of literacy.

JANET WONG'S POETRY

Janet Wong's first two poetry collections, *Good Luck Gold and Other Poems* (Simon & Schuster, 1994) and *A Suitcase of Seaweed, and Other Poems* (Simon & Schuster, 1996) focus on her own background, exploring cultural connections and growing up with Korean and Chinese traditions. Many of the poems in these two collections lend themselves to poetry performance. For example, try "Face It" (*A Suitcase of Seaweed*) with three stanzas that reflect the writer's musings on her nose, her eyes, and her mouth and how each represents a different part of her identity. Three groups could each read a different stanza, using motions to point to each body part in turn. In "Speak Up," Wong uses spacing to indicate the two speaking roles in the poem. Here many voices could read the left side of the poem representing a group of questioning children, while a solo voice (perhaps the adult) responds with the right side of the poem expressing the immigrant child's point of view.

In addition, Wong has explored these experiences further in several picture books: *This Next New Year* (Farrar, Straus & Giroux, 2000), *The Trip Back Home* (Harcourt, 2000), and *Apple Pie 4th of July* (Harcourt, 2001). Together, they provide a fascinating view of a child's experience growing up in the U.S. with roots in another country. Poems like "Face It" and "Speak Up" address directly what it feels like to be an American, but "different." Be open to children sharing their own experiences with culture and identity in their own lives. Link these books with Jorge Argueta's *Movie in My Pillow/Una pelicula en mi almohada* (Children's Book Press, 2001) or Monica Gunning's *America, My New Home* (Boyds Mills Press, 2004) for additional perspectives.

Wong also has authored several poetry collections on a variety of other topics. *Behind the Wheel: Poems about Driving* (Simon & Schuster, 1999) is a wonderful gift for a teenager who is learning to drive. *The Rainbow Hand: Poems about Mothers and Children* (Simon & Schuster, 2000) is an homage to mothers and our relationships with them and includes perfect "Mother's Day" poem tributes. Connect this selection with Pat Mora's collection, *Love to Mama: A Celebration of Mothers* (Lee and Low, 2001). What other milestones or occasions are coming up that provide an opportunity for sharing or writing poetry? Children can try composing tribute poems in honor of their mothers or other special individuals in their lives.

Children are often intrigued by and sometimes afraid of the world of dreams and superstitions. Wong has two collections of poems that address these particular areas: *Night Garden: Poems from the World of Dreams* (Simon & Schuster, 2000) and *Knock on Wood: Poems about Superstitions* (Simon & Schuster, 2003). Both are beautifully illustrated by Julie Paschkis and invite children to express their own beliefs and concerns—perhaps poetically. For children who want to try writing, Janet Wong also has an engaging picture book resource, *You Have to Write* (Simon & Schuster, 2002) that they will enjoy and find helpful. Perhaps children could interview family members to investigate other superstitions held in the family and illustrate one or create a poem about it. For an additional resource, look for Alvin Schwartz's collection of American folk beliefs, *Cross your Fingers, Spit in your Hat: Superstitions and Other Beliefs* (HarperCollins, 1974).

For the intriguing topic of dreams, share a parallel book of poetry by Francisco X. Alarcón, *Poems to Dream Together/Poemas Para Soñar Juntos* (Lee and Low, 2005). His focus is on dreams and goals for the future, rather than nighttime dreams, which offers another extension of the dream topic. And for further connections, children can research the tradition of the Native American dream catcher and share findings or examples with the group.

Valerie Worth

VALERIE WORTH'S POETRY

Beginning with her first collection published in 1972, Valerie Worth offered beautiful, spartan, free verse poems for children often used to a diet of strong rhyme. For one collection which includes all 99 of her original four "small" poems plus more, look for *All the Small Poems and Fourteen More* (Farrar, Straus & Giroux, 1996). Worth's gift is to show us a variety of ordinary subjects—garbage, clock, safety pin, lawnmower, magnet, library, and coat hangers—with extraordinary freshness and precision. Accompanying each poem is a perfectly placed pen-and-ink sketch by Natalie Babbitt, a notable author in her own right. Children may enjoy reading some of Babbitt's novels that include her unique illustrations like *Bub: Or the Very Best Thing* (Harper-Collins, 1996) or *Nellie, A Cat on Her Own* (Farrar, Straus & Giroux, 1992).

To seek out Worth's original "small poem" collections, look for:

Small Poems (Farrar, Straus & Giroux, 1972)

More Small Poems (Farrar, Straus & Giroux, 1976)

Still More Small Poems (Farrar, Straus & Giroux, 1978)

Small Poems Again (Farrar, Straus & Giroux, 1985)

All the Small Poems (Farrar, Straus & Giroux, 1987)

Children may enjoy the small trim size of these books and want to create their own small books. What other small-sized books are they familiar with? Beatrix Potter's *The Tale of Peter Rabbit* (Warne, 2002)? Mercer and Marianna Mayer's *A Boy, a Dog, a Frog, and a Friend* (Dial, 2003)? They can create a display of small books, small poems, and small objects for small children.

Valerie Worth's poems can also be combined with classic poems often studied in school. A contemporary poem can offer a bridge to understanding an older, classic poem. Or for students who are already familiar with the classic poems, it can provide a basis for comparison and discussion. For example, William Blake's classic poem, "The Tyger" can be paired with Valerie Worth's poem, "Tiger" found in *The 20th Century Children's Poetry Treasury* (Knopf, 1999). Or Carl Sandburg's classic poem, "Fog" can be paired with Worth's poem, "Frost" (*All the Small Poems and Fourteen More*). Children can create a mini-poster featuring both poems along with a drawing combining images of both.

Worth has other poetry collections worth sharing, including *Peacock and Other Poems* (Farrar, Straus & Giroux, 2002) which is similar in style to the "Small" collections focused on animals and objects. Together, all these works offer powerful examples of similes, personification, and structure. Connect them with the poetry of Eve Merriam and Myra Cohn Livingston for a rich poetry unit.

Valerie Worth departed from this small-scale format with the poetry book, *At Christmastime* (HarperCollins, 1992), a large picture book with vivid full-page color illustrations by Antonio Frasconi. Obviously, these poems are perfect for sharing at Christmas celebrations, but also include non-religious topics for the holiday season, as well. Consider adding Anna Grossnickle Hines's poetry book, *Winter Lights: A Season in Poems & Quilts* (Greenwillow, 2005), or *Hold Christmas in Your Heart: African American Songs, Poems, and Stories for the Holidays* by Cheryl Willis Hudson (Scholastic, 2002), or *The Stable Rat and Other Christmas Poems* by Julia Cunningham (Greenwillow, 2001) for other winter holiday perspectives. Children can choose a favorite holiday poem and create a card or ornament featuring that verse.

Animal Poems (Farrar, Straus Giroux, 2007) is another picture book collection of Worth's poetry that is colorfully illustrated—this time by collage artist Steve Jenkins. These animal poems are wonderful introductions to Worth's gift for description and metaphor. Match them with Michio Mado's poetry in *The Animals* (McElderry, 1992) or Douglas Florian's work in *Mammalabilia* (Harcourt, 2000). Gather nonfiction books about animals for contrasting both the art and photographs, the poetry and prose. Children can create their own collage or cut paper animal pictures and write or choose animal poems to accompany them.

Finally, for readers who love the physicality of books—the cover, the paper, the ink, etc.—Worth's poem "library" is a tribute to those special qualities (from *All the Small Poems and Fourteen More)*. It is also a wonderful example of poetry that doesn't rhyme, but still has an inviting rhythm and structure and the perfect choice for extending a welcome to the library with her words, "Listen to the / Silent twitter / Of a billion / Tiny busy / Black words."

Jane Yolen

http://www.janeyolen.com

JANE YOLEN'S POETRY

Jane Yolen's love of rhyme and language is evident in many of her picture books as well as her poetry collections. For example, her hilarious "How Do Dinosaurs" picture books illustrated by Mark Teague are told through infectious rhymes that delight young children. She has also published over 30 collections of poetry including lullabies and nursery rhymes, poems about nature and animals, and anthologies of poems by other writers.

Jane Yolen has several poetry compilations ideally suited to sharing with young children including her *Mother Goose Songbook* (Boyds Mill Press, 1992) which celebrates traditional rhymes and songs, *The Lullaby Songbook* (Harcourt, 1986) which includes a variety of songs from spirituals to Yiddish cradle songs, and *Street Rhymes Around the World* (Boyds Mills, 1992) and *Sleep Rhymes Around the World* (Boyds Mills/Wordsong, 1994), two international, multilingual collections of verse to learn and recite. These could be linked with other similar collections of Spanish nursery rhymes by José-Luis Orozco such as *De Colores and Other Latin-American Folk Songs for Children* (Dutton, 1994) or Chinese traditional rhymes such as Mingfong Ho's *Maples in the Mist: Children's Poems from the Tang Dynasty* (Lothrop, 1996).

For a fun twist on the traditional story of "The Three Bears," look for Yolen's *The Three Bears Rhyme Book* (Harcourt Brace, 1987), a collection of rhyming poems from the point of view of Baby Bear, or *The Three Bears Holiday Rhyme Book* (Harcourt, 1995), Baby Bear's holiday rhyme collection. Connect these with any previous version of the folktale or with other bear poems, like Alice Schertle's *Teddy Bear, Teddy Bear* (HarperCollins, 2003). For another twist on these and other folktale characters, look for Alan and Janet Ahlberg's *The Jolly Postman* (reissued by Little, Brown, 2006).

Perhaps one of Jane Yolen's major contributions to children's poetry has been her nature poetry collections, including two anthologies she compiled, *Mother Earth, Father Sky: Poems of Our Planet* (Boyds Mills Press, 1996) and *Weather Report* (Boyds Mills Press, 1993) and her own nature poetry writing which includes: *Ring of Earth: A Child's Book of Seasons* (Harcourt Brace, 1986), *Horizons: Poems As Far As the Eye Can See* (Wordsong/Boyds Mills Press, 2002), *What Rhymes with Moon?* (Philomel, 1993), and *Color Me a Rhyme: Nature Poems for Young People* (Wordsong/Boyds Mills Press, 2000). These collected works offer a multitude of poems to connect with Earth Day celebrations, bad weather days, first days of the season, lunar eclipses, and the like. The color poems, in particular, can serve as inspiration for studying color in natural objects like fruits, vegetables, leaves, and rocks and then composing descriptive poems. Use Bruce McMillan's *Growing Colors* (HarperTrophy, 1994) and Lois Ehlert's *Eating the Alphabet* (Voyager, 1993) as additional resource books and Mary O'Neill's *Hailstones and Halibut Bones* (Doubleday, 1989) for more examples of color poems.

Three of Yolen's poetry collections look at water in its varying forms: *Once upon Ice and Other Frozen Poems* (Boyds Mills Press, 1997), *Snow, Snow: Winter Poems for Children* (Boyds Mills Press, 1998) and *Water Music: Poems for Children* (Boyds Mills, 1995), all illustrated with stunning photographs taken by her son, Jason Stemple. For more "wet" poetry, consult Joan Bransfield Graham's *Splish Splash* (Houghton Mifflin, 2001) and Constance Levy's *Splash! Poems of Our Watery World* (Orchard, 2002). Many of these water poems lend themselves to reading aloud along with props such as soap bubbles, Christmas tree "icicles," or audiotapes of waterfalls or the ocean surf.

Jane Yolen often writes poetry about animals in compilations such as *Alphabestiary: Animal Poems from A to Z* (Boyds Mills Press, 1994), *The Originals: Animals That Time Forgot* (Philomel Books, 1998), *Sea Watch: A Book of Poetry* (Putnam, 1996), and *Least Things: Poems about Small Natures* (Boyds Mills Press, 2003), and *Raining Cats and Dogs* (Harcourt, 1993). She has three collections of poetry about birds, in particular: *Bird Watch* (Philomel, 1990), *Wild Wings: Poems for Young People* (Boyds Mills Press, 2002), and *Fine Feathered Friends: Poems for Young People* (Boyds Mills, 2004). Combine these with the animal poetry of Avis Harley, J. Patrick Lewis, Douglas Florian, and Joyce Sidman for a totally animal poetry unit.

There is even a professional resource available for using Jane Yolen's poetry with children entitled *Poetry Play Any Day with Jane Yolen* by Cheryl Potts (Upstart Books, 1999). This book includes activities, educational games, and simple craft projects to promote poetry with children via Yolen's work.

Jane Yolen maintains an active Web site at http://www.janeyolen.com that lists her works along with her comments about each one. The site also includes information about her awards, teaching, her family, her friends, and a call for educators to add their ideas to the site. She also answers questions that young readers frequently ask her. Children who enjoy her poems may enjoy commenting on her Web site or contacting her directly.

More Poets

POETS TO WATCH

Here are individuals who are emerging as notable poets writing for children.

Adoff, Jaime
Burg, Brad
Cyrus, Kurt
Ghigna, Charles
Grandits, John
Greenberg, David
Johnson, Lindsay Lee
Katz, Alan
Kay, Verla
Lawson, JonArno
Medina, Jane
Mitton, Tony

Mordhorst, Heidi
Moss, Jeff
Nesbitt, Kenn
Nicola-Lisa, W.
Paul, Ann Whitford
Pomerantz, Charlotte
Rex, Adam
Roemer, Heidi
Smith, Hope Anita
Van Meter, Gretchen
Wolf, Allan
Zimmer, Tracie Vaughn

PEOPLE WHO WRITE OTHER THINGS PLUS POETRY

There are many writers who have established a reputation for writing award-winning fiction and/or nonfiction and who also write quality poetry for children.

Brenner, Barbara
Bruchac, Joseph
Bryan, Ashley

Calmenson, Stephanie
Cofer, Judith Ortiz
Dahl, Roald

Havill, Juanita
Ho, Mingfong
Hubbell, Patricia
Johnson, Angela
Johnston, Tony
Joseph, Lynn
Little, Jean
Lyon, George Ella
Myers, Walter Dean
Pearson, Susan

Ryder, Joanne
Rylant, Cynthia
Scieszka, Jon
Sierra, Judy
Spinelli, Eileen
Stevenson, James
Turner, Ann
Updike, Judy
Winter, Jonah
Wood, Nancy

VERSE NOVELISTS

The novel in verse is a poetic form that many new writers are trying, and these authors, in particular, have created novels that are truly poetic.

Creech, Sharon
Crist-Evans, Craig
Glenn, Mel
Grover, Lorie Ann
Hemphill, Stephanie
Herrick, Steven
Hesse, Karen

Koertge, Ron
Levithan, David
Nelson, Marilyn
Sones, Sonya
Testa, Maria
Wayland, April Halprin
Wolff, Virginia Euwer

ANTHOLOGISTS

Although some of these individuals create their own original poetry and write in other genres, they are known for producing well-regarded anthologies of poetry that include the works of many voices.

Agard, John
Carlson, Lori
Cole, William
Franco, Betsy
Gordon, Ruth
Jones, Hettie
Lansky, Bruce
Larrick, Nancy
McNaughton, Colin

Nichols, Grace
Philip, Neil
Rogasky, Barbara
Rosen, Michael
Rosenberg, Liz
Sneve, Virginia Driving Hawk
Sullivan, Charles
Vecchione, Patricia

CLASSIC POETS

These are poets whose works were most familiar to readers of previous generations. However, many of their poems hold timeless appeal and frequently appear in anthologies today.

Behn, Harry
Belloc, Hilaire
Blake, William
Bodecker, N. M.
Bontemps, Arna
Brooks, Gwendolyn
Carroll, Lewis
Clifton, Lucille
Coatsworth, Elizabeth
Cullen, Countee
de la Mare, Walter
Dickinson, Emily
Dunbar, Paul Laurence
Farjeon, Eleanor

Field, Eugene
Frost, Robert
Holman, Felice
Hughes, Langston
Kipling, Rudyard
Lear, Edward
Lindsay, Vachel
Longfellow, Henry Wadsworth
Milne, A.A.
Richards, Laura E.
Rossetti, Christina
Sandburg, Carl
Stevenson, Robert Louis
Zolotow, Charlotte

POETS WHO WRITE FOR ADULTS, PLUS CHILDREN

Several poets write poetry primarily for adults, and also create poetry for children.

Hirsch, Robin
Hughes, Ted
Kumin, Maxine

Troupe, Quincy
Wilbur, Richard

*A note about categories. These categories are not absolute and many poets fit in more than one place. Pigeonholing poets is precarious, since poets are known for innovation and experimentation. These lists are intended only as a guide to finding more poets and poetry sharing. In fact, many of the poets profiled individually also create anthologies, or write verse novels, or publish in other genres. In addition, new poets are emerging all the time in anthologies and in individual collections, so keep a watchful eye for new voices not yet featured here.

Awards for Poetry for Young People

THE NCTE AWARD FOR EXCELLENCE IN POETRY FOR CHILDREN

The National Council of Teachers of English established its Award for Excellence in Poetry for Children in 1977 to honor a living American poet for his or her lifetime achievement in works for children ages 3–13. The award was given annually until 1982, after which it was decided that the award would be given every three years.
Web site: http://www.ncte.org/about/awards/sect/elem/106857.htm.

Recipients

2006	Nikki Grimes	1985	Lilian Moore
2003	Mary Ann Hoberman	1982	John Ciardi
2000	X. J. Kennedy	1981	Eve Merriam
1997	Eloise Greenfield	1980	Myra Cohn Livingston
1994	Barbara Esbensen	1979	Karla Kuskin
1991	Valerie Worth	1978	Aileen Fisher
1988	Arnold Adoff	1977	David McCord

CHILDREN'S POET LAUREATE

The Children's Poet Laureate award was established by the Poetry Foundation in 2006 to raise awareness of the fact that children have a natural receptivity to poetry and are its most appreciative audience, especially when poems are written specifically for them. The Children's Poet Laureate receives a $25,000 cash prize and a medallion, which includes the inscription "Permit a child to join" taken from an Emily Dickinson poem. The Children's Poet Laureate serves as a consultant to the Foundation for a two-year period and gives at least two major public readings for children and their families, teachers, and librarians during his/her term. He/she will also serve as an advisor to the Poetry Foundation on children's literature, and may engage in a variety of projects and events to help instill a love of poetry among the nation's youngest readers.

Web site: http://www.poetryfoundation.org/.

Recipient

2006   Jack Prelutsky

LEE BENNETT HOPKINS/International Reading Association PROMISING POET AWARD

The Lee Bennett Hopkins/International Reading Association Promising Poet Award was established by Hopkins along with the International Reading Association in 1995 to encourage new poets in their writing. These poets have only published two books (to qualify for the award), but their work has already been judged to be of high quality. The award is given every three years.

Web site: http://www.reading.org/association/awards/childrens_hopkins.html.

Recipients

2004   Lindsay Lee Johnson
2001   Craig Crist-Evans
1998   Kristine O'Connell George
1995   Deborah Chandra

LEE BENNETT HOPKINS POETRY AWARD

The Lee Bennett Hopkins award established in 1993 is presented annually to an American poet or anthologist for the most outstanding new book of children's poetry published in the previous calendar year.

Web site: http://www.pabook.libraries.psu.edu/activities/hopkins/index.html.

Recipients

2006 *Jazz* by Walter Dean Myers (Holiday House)
2005 *Song of the Water Boatman and Other Pond Poems* by Joyce Sidman (Houghton Mifflin)
2004 *Here in Harlem* by Walter Dean Myers (Holiday House)
2003 *The Wishing Bone and Other Poems* by Stephen Mitchell (Candlewick)
2002 *Splash! Poems of our Watery World* by Constance Levy (Orchard)
2001 *Pieces: A Year in Poems and Quilts* by Anna Grossnickle Hines (Greenwillow)
2000 *Light-Gathering Poems* by Liz Rosenberg (Henry Holt)
1999 *What Have You Lost?* by Naomi Shihab Nye (Greenwillow)
1998 *The Other Side* by Angela Johnson (Orchard)
1997 *The Great Frog Race* by Kristine O'Connell George (Clarion)
1996 *Voices from the Wild* by David Bouchard (Chronicle)
1995 *Dance with Me* by Barbara Esbensen (HarperCollins)
1994 *Beast Feast* by Douglas Florian (Harcourt)
1993 *Spirit Walker* by Nancy Wood (Doubleday)
1992 *Sing to the Sun* by Ashley Bryan (HarperCollins)

THE CLAUDIA LEWIS AWARD

The Claudia Lewis Award is given by Bank Street College in New York. The award is given annually for the best poetry book of the year in honor of the late Claudia Lewis, a distinguished children's book expert and longtime member of the Bank Street College faculty and Children's Book Committee. Web site: http://www.bankstreet.edu/bookcom/about_awards.html.

Recipients

2005 *A Kick in the Head: An Everyday Guide to Poetic Forms* selected by Paul B. Janeczko (Candlewick Press)
2004 *Here in Harlem: Poems in Many Voices* by Walter Dean Myers (Holiday House)
      Hummingbird Nest: A Journal of Poems by Kristine O'Connell George (Tricycle Press)
2003 *The Way a Door Closes* by Hope Anita Smith (Henry Holt Books)
      Yesterday I had the Blues by Jeron Ashford Frame (Tricycle Press)
2002 *Little Dog and Duncan* by Kristine O'Connell George (Clarion)
2001 *Love that Dog* by Sharon Creech (HarperCollins)
      Amber was Brave, Essie was Smart Vera B. Williams (Greenwillow)
2000 *Mammalabilia* by Douglas Florian (Harcourt)

1999 *Stop Pretending* by Sonya Sones (HarperCollins)
1998 *I, too, Sing America* by Catherine Clinton (Houghton Mifflin)
1997 *The Invisible Ladder* edited by Liz Rosenberg (Henry Holt)

Calendar of Poet Birthdays

JANUARY

2   Jean Little
5   Monica Gunning
6   Carl Sandburg
7   Minfong Ho
6   Carl Sandburg
18 A. A. Milne; Grace Nichols

19 Pat Mora; Edgar Allan Poe; Effie Lee Newsom
25 Robert Burns
27 Lewis Carroll
29 Tony Johnston

FEBRUARY

1   Langston Hughes
2   Judith Viorst
3   Liz Rosenberg
11 Jane Yolen
13 Carole Boston Weatherford

15 Sonya Sones
20 Kenn Nesbitt
21 Francisco X. Alarcón
26 Allan Wolf
27 Laura E. Richards

MARCH

1   Alan Katz
4   Craig Crist-Evans
9   Robert Pottle
12 Naomi Shihab Nye

13 David Harrison
17 Lilian Moore; Ralph Fletcher
18 Douglas Florian
26 Robert Frost

APRIL

7	Alice Schertle	22	William Jay Smith; Ron Koertge
12	Gary Soto	25	George Ella Lyon
13	Lee Bennett Hopkins	26	Marilyn Nelson
20	April Halprin Wayland	28	Barbara Juster Esbensen

MAY

2	Bobbi Katz	8	Constance Levy
5	J. Patrick Lewis	10	Mel Glenn
6	Kristine O'Connell George; José-Luis Orozco	12	Edward Lear
7	Michael Rosen	17	Eloise Greenfield
		25	Joyce Carol Thomas

JUNE

1	Bruce Lansky	16	Kalli Dakos
6	Nancy Willard; Cynthia Rylant	20	Nancy Wood
7	Nikki Giovanni	24	John Ciardi
8	Judy Sierra	26	Nancy Willard

JULY

6	Kathi Appelt	16	Arnold Adoff
10	Rebecca Kai Dotlich; Patricia Hubbell	17	Karla Kuskin
13	Anna Grossnickle Hines	19	Eve Merriam
		27	Paul Janeczko

AUGUST

12	Mary Ann Hoberman; Walter Dean Myers	19	Ogden Nash
15	Betsy Franco	21	X.J. Kennedy
17	Myra Cohn Livingston	29	Karen Hesse; Sylvia Cassedy
		31	Dennis Lee

SEPTEMBER

3   Helen Frost
5   Paul Fleischman
8   Jack Prelutsky
9   Aileen Fisher

15   Sara Holbrook
25   Harry Behn; Shel Silverstein
30   Janet S. Wong

OCTOBER

3   Marilyn Singer
20   Nikki Grimes
27   Lillian Morrison

29   Valerie Worth
31   Joan Bransfield Graham

NOVEMBER

2   Ted Scheu
13   Robert Louis Stevenson
15   David McCord

18   Robin Hirsch
22   Brod Bagert

DECEMBER

1   Carol Diggory Shields
5   Christina Rossetti
10   Emily Dickinson
13   Georgia Heard

21   Susan Pearson
27   Juan Felipe Herrera
30   Rudyard Kipling

Poet Promotion Activities

Featuring a "poet of the month" or hosting a real or "virtual" visiting poet are two excellent ways to showcase the people behind the poems we enjoy. Choosing a variety of poets to highlight on a rotating basis can provide children with more in-depth exposure to their poems and poetry writing. Here are guidelines for creating such a "featured poet" center:

- Collect the poet's works and make them prominent and available.
- Create a bulletin board, poster, or display featuring the poet (include a photo, a print out of their Web site home page, a few "fun facts" about their lives).
- Read the poets' works aloud often.
- Look up biographical information about the poet and share it with children.
- Look for autobiographies, video/audio interviews, and poet Web sites to share.
- Investigate setting up an online chat with or even a guest appearance by a poet; be sure to prepare the children beforehand with extensive reading.
- If funds allow, consider setting up a Poet-in-Residence program, inviting a poet to work with children on an ongoing basis for a short period of time.
- Involve children in choosing poets to study and in developing featured poet centers.

We typically feature popular fiction writers with book talks and displays in our book promotion activities, but have we considered giving poets the same publicity and close study? Creating time and space for featured poets helps introduce their work and encourage children to read more poetry. In addition, it can be inspiring for young would-be poets to see that there are successful adults who have made poetry writing their career.

How to Share Poetry

Many people are reluctant to share poetry because they don't feel knowledgeable about which poems to choose or comfortable about how to share them. This book is designed to combat the first obstacle, in particular. The information provided here should be helpful for knowing which poets and poetry books to select. Then what? Some suggestions for sharing poems are included in the information about each poet as a beginning point. In a nutshell, the philosophy underlying this book is that the best way to share poetry with children is orally, read aloud by an enthusiastic adult, incorporating as many opportunities for children to participate in the oral reading as possible. Poems can serve as the opening routine to a story time or lesson or as a closing moment at the end. A poem can be linked with a story or other activity, or poems can serve as the entire focus of the time together.

And what do we do after sharing a poem? Often the best thing to do is to read it aloud again—and invite children to participate in that reading aloud in some way. If time allows, discussing, drawing, dramatizing, and more reading are all excellent follow-up activities. And for some children, writing poetry is a natural extension of poetry sharing and reading. However, only a small proportion of children are generally going to want to be writers or poets when they grow up. All children can enjoy poetry, have fun with rhymes and humor, and build their language and vocabulary knowledge. Children who hear poems read aloud regularly have a foundation of rhyme and word knowledge to build upon as they become literate adults, as well as a reservoir of ideas and emotions expressed through poetry to draw from throughout their lives.

Poet Biographies, Autobiographies and Memoirs

These books share information about the lives of poets and how they came to write poetry.

Bedard, Michael. 1992. *Emily*. Illustrated by Barbara Cooney. New Haven, CT: Lester Publishing.

Bober, Natalie S. 1991. *A Restless Spirit: The Story of Robert Frost*. New York: Henry Holt.

Burleigh, Robert. 2004. *Langston's Train Ride*. Illustrated by Leonard Jenkins. New York:Scholastic.

Christensen, Bonnie. 2001. *Woody Guthrie: Poet of the People*. New York: Knopf.

Cooper, Floyd. 1994. *Coming Home: From the Life of Langston Hughes*. New York: Philomel.

Florian, Douglas. 2006. *See for Your Self*. Katonah, NY: Richard C. Owen Publishers.

Gherman, Beverly. 1996. *Robert Louis Stevenson, Teller of Tales*. New York: Atheneum.

Harrison, David. 2004. *Connecting Dots: Poems of My Journey*. Honesdale, PA: Boyds Mills Press.

Hopkins, Lee Bennett. 1993. *The Writing Bug*. Katonah, NY: Richard C. Owen Publishers.

——. 1995. *Been to Yesterdays: Poems of a Life*. Illustrated by Charlene Rendeiro. Honesdale, PA: Wordsong/Boyds Mills Press.

Josephson, Judith Pinkerton. 2000. *Nikki Giovanni, Poet of the People*. Berkeley Heights, NJ: Enslow.

Kerley, Barbara. 2004. *Walt Whitman: Words for America*. Illustrated by Brian Selznick. New York: Scholastic.

Kuskin, Karla. 1995. *Thoughts, Pictures, and Words*. Photographs by Nicholas Kuskin. Katonah, NY: Richard C. Owen Publishers.

Lasky, Kathryn. 2003. *A Voice of Her Own: The Story of Phillis Wheatley, Slave Poet*. Illustrated by Paul Lee. Cambridge, MA: Candlewick.

Lewis, J. Patrick. 2000. *Freedom Like Sunlight: Praise songs for Black Americans*. Illustrated by John Thompson. North Mankato, MN: Creative Editions.

McKissack, Patricia C. 1984. *Paul Laurence Dunbar, A Poet to Remember*. New York: Children's Press.

Meltzer, Milton. 1997. *Langston Hughes: A Biography*. Illustrated by Stephen Alcorn. Minneapolis, MN: Millbrook.

——. 1999. *Carl Sandburg: A Biography*. Minneapolis, MN: Twenty-First Century Books.

——. 2002. *Walt Whitman: A Biography*. Minneapolis, MN: Twenty-First Century Books.

——. 2004. *Emily Dickinson: A Biography*. Minneapolis, MN: Twenty-First Century Books.

Murphy, Jim. 1993. *Across America on an Emigrant Train*. New York: Clarion.

Niven, Penelope. 2003. *Carl Sandburg: Adventures of a Poet*. Illustrated by Marc Nadel. San Diego, CA: Harcourt Brace.

Osofsky, Audrey. 1996. *Free to Dream: The Making of a Poet: Langston Hughes*. New York: Lothrop, Lee & Shepard.

Perdomo, Willie. 2002. *Visiting Langston*. Illustrated by Bryan Collier. New York: Henry Holt.

Reef, Catherine. 2000. *Paul Laurence Dunbar: Portrait of a Poet*. Berkeley Heights, NJ: Enslow.

——. 1995. *Walt Whitman*. New York: Clarion Books.

Strickland, Michael R. 1996. *African-American Poets*. Berkeley Heights, NJ: Enslow.

Strong, Amy. 2003. *Lee Bennett Hopkins: A Children's Poet*. New York: Franklin Watts.

Winter, Jeanette. 2002. *Emily Dickinson's Letters to the World*. New York: Frances Foster Books/Farrar, Straus & Giroux.

Popular Poetry Web Sites

THE ACADEMY OF AMERICAN POETS
http://www.poets.org

This site offers poet biographies, sample poems, audio archives, National Poetry Month celebrations, curriculum resources, teacher discussion forums, teaching tips, and more. Of particular interest, is a listing of "success stories" describing various poetry promotion activities.

POET'S CORNER
http://www.theotherpages.org/poems/

This site includes the full text of several thousand poems published in some form or other before 1923 in the United States. and thus in the public domain. The site includes a helpful author, title, and subject index for searching poems, too. Many classic poems for children are available here.

POETRY 180
http://www.loc.gov/poetry/180/

Billy Collins, former U.S. poet laureate, helped create this site to make it easy for high school students to hear or read a poem on each of the 180 days of the school year. He suggests reading the poems following the end of daily announcements over the public address system. Many contemporary poems are provided here and may be appropriate for middle-grade children.

POETRY DAILY
http://www.poems.com/

This is a wonderful resource for enjoying a new poem every day, although these are not poems for children, per se. It's a helpful professional source of poetry each day, something you can tap into on a regular basis to feed your own poetic muse.

GIGGLE POETRY
http://www.gigglepoetry.com/

This kid-friendly Web site offers poems to read, with new ones posted regularly, as well as opportunities for child interaction. Kids can rate the poems, enter poetry writing contests, explore fun pages for poetry reading, etc. There are also resource activities for adults who share poetry with children.

INTERNET SCHOOL LIBRARY MEDIA CENTER (ISLMC) POETRY FOR CHILDREN
http://falcon.jmu.edu/~ramseyil/poechild.htm

This site is particularly helpful for adults, rather than children, and provides information about forms of poetry, many teaching units and activities, some e-texts and bibliographies, and children's songs and music of all kinds.

THE LIBRARY OF CONGRESS POETRY AND LITERATURE CENTER
http://www.loc.gov/poetry/

This site may interest older children who are interested in learning about the Poet Laureates of the United States, national prizes in poetry, special poetry events, and the archive of recordings of over 2000 adult poets reading their own work.

FAVORITE POEM PROJECT
http://www.favoritepoem.org/

This site features Poet Laureate Robert Pinsky's project to have average citizens audiotape their favorite poems.

POETRY HILL POETRY
http://www.potatohill.com

This site is rich with ideas for sharing poems and poetry writing with children of all ages, including poetry-writing contests for kids, poems written by children of all ages, and teacher resources and workshop information.

MAGNETIC POETRY
http://www.magneticpoetry.com/

Here you will find a multitude of kit options including Shakespeare, haiku, and foreign language kits, as well as kits designed especially for children. It also offers the opportunity to publish poetry created by adult or child "magnetic" poets.

CHILDREN'S BOOK COUNCIL YOUNG PEOPLE'S POETRY WEEK
http://www.cbcbooks.org/yppw/

The Children's Book Council produces promotional materials developed especially for celebrating Young People's Poetry Week, including posters, postcards, and bookmarks. Their Web site also provides helpful articles and activities.

Poetry Anthologies

There are many, many wonderful poetry anthologies published for children, full of poems by different poets. This book is largely focused on highlighting individual poem collections by individual poets, but poems by these poets also appear regularly in general poetry anthologies. In addition new poets often appear *first* in anthologies before publishing their own individual collections of poetry. Here is a beginning list of poetry anthologies that include quality works by wonderful poets gathered in a variety of interesting themes and topics.

Brenner, Barbara, comp. 1994. *The Earth is Painted Green: A Garden of Poems about Our Planet.* New York: Scholastic.

———, comp. 2000. *Voices: Poetry and Art from Around the World.* Washington, DC: National Geographic Society.

Clinton, Catherine, comp. 1993/1998. *I, Too, Sing America: Three Centuries of African American Poetry.* Boston: Houghton Mifflin.

Cohn, Amy L., comp. 1993. *From Sea to Shining Sea: A Treasury of American Folklore and Folk Songs.* New York: Scholastic.

Cullinan, Bernice F., ed. 1996. *A Jar of Tiny Stars: Poems by NCTE Award-winning Poets.* Honesdale, PA: Wordsong/Boyds Mills Press.

De Regniers, Beatrice Schenk, Moore, Eva, White, Mary Michaels, and Carr, Jan, eds. 1988. *Sing a Song of Popcorn: Every Child's Book of Poems.* New York: Scholastic.

Ho, Mingfong, translator and compiler. 1996. *Maples in the Mist: Children's Poems from the Tang Dynasty.* New York: Lothrop.

Hopkins, Lee Bennett, comp. 2005. *Days to Celebrate: A Full Year of Poetry, People, Holidays, History, Fascinating Facts, and More.* New York: Greenwillow.

Hudson, Wade, comp. 1993. *Pass It On: African American Poetry for Children.* New York: Scholastic.

Janeczko, Paul, comp. 2002. *Seeing the Blue Between: Advice and Inspiration for Young Poets.* Cambridge, MA: Candlewick.

Kennedy, X.J and Kennedy, Dorothy, comp. 1982. *Knock at a Star: A Child's Introduction to Poetry.* Boston: Little Brown.

Lansky, Bruce, comp. 1994. *A Bad Case of the Giggles: Kid's Favorite Funny Poems*. Deephaven, MN: Meadowbrook Press.

Mora, Pat, comp. 2001. *Love to Mama: A Tribute to Mothers*. New York: Lee & Low Books.

Nye, Naomi Shihab, comp. 1992. *This Same Sky: A Collection of Poems from Around the World*. New York: Four Winds Press.

Panzer, Nora, ed. 1994. *Celebrate America in Poetry and Art*. New York: Hyperion.

Prelutsky, Jack, comp. 1997. *The Beauty of the Beast*. New York: Knopf.

——, comp. 1983. *The Random House Book of Poetry for Children*. New York: Random House.

——, comp. 1999. *The 20th Century Children's Poetry Treasury*. New York: Knopf.

Rich, Mary Perrotta, ed. 1998. *Book Poems: Poems from National Children's Book Week, 1959–1998*. New York: Children's Book Council.

Rochelle, Belinda, comp. 2001. *Words with Wings: A Treasury of African-American Poetry and Art*. New York: HarperCollins.

Schwartz, Alvin. 1992. *And the Green Grass Grew All Around: Folk Poetry from Everyone*. New York: HarperCollins.

Sierra, Judy. 2005. *Schoolyard Rhymes: Kids' Own Rhymes for Rope Skipping, Hand Clapping, Ball Bouncing, and Just Plain Fun*. New York: Knopf.

Sullivan, Charles, ed. 1994. *Here is My Kingdom: Hispanic-American Literature and Art for Young People*. New York: H.N. Abrams.

Tashjian, Virginia, comp. 1995. *Juba This and Juba That: Story Hour Stretches for Large or Small Groups*. Boston, MA: Little, Brown.

Volavkova, Hana, ed. 1993. *I Never Saw Another Butterfly: Children's Drawings and Poems from Terezin Concentration Camp 1942–1944*. New York: Schocken Books.

Westcott, Nadine Bernard, comp. 1994. *Never Take a Pig to Lunch and Other Poems about the Fun of Eating*. New York: Orchard.

Whipple, Laura, comp. 1989. *Eric Carle's Animals, Animals*. New York: Scholastic.

——, comp. 1994. *Celebrating America: A Collection of Poems and Images of the American Spirit*. New York: Philomel Books.

Poems about Libraries and Reading

Appelt, Kathi. 1997. "Javier," from *Just People and Paper/Pen/Poem: A Young Writer's Way to Begin*. Spring, TX: Absey & Co.

Bagert, Brod. 1999. "Library-Gold," from *Rainbows, Head Lice and Pea-Green Tile; Poems in the Voice of the Classroom Teacher*. Gainesville, FL: Maupin House.

Dakos, Kalli. 2003. "When the Librarian Reads to Us," from *Put Your Eyes Up Here: And Other School Poems*. New York: Simon & Schuster.

Frost, Helen. 2003. "Do Not Leave Children Unattended," from *Keesha's House*. New York: Farrar, Straus & Giroux.

George, Kristine O'Connell. 2002. "School Librarian," from *Swimming Upstream: Middle School Poems*. New York: Clarion Books.

Giovanni, Nikki. 1971. "ten years old," from *Spin a Soft Black Song*. New York: Hill & Wang.

Glenn, Mel. 2000. "Eddie Sabinsky," from *Split Image*. New York: HarperCollins.

Greenfield. Eloise. 2006. "At the Library," from *The Friendly Four*. New York: HarperCollins.

Grimes, Nikki. 1997. "At the Library," from *It's Raining Laughter*. New York: Dial.

——. 1998. "42nd Street Library" form *Jazmin's Notebook*. New York: Dial.

Gunning, Monica. 2004. "The Library," from *America, My New Home*. Honesdale, PA: Wordsong/Boyds Mills Press.

Herrick, Steven. 2004. "Lord of the Lounge," from *The Simple Gift*. New York: Simon & Schuster.

Hopkins, Ellen. 2006. "See, the Library," from *burned*. New York: Margaret K. McElderry Books.

Katz, Alan. 2001. 'Give Me a Break," from *Take Me Out of the Bathtub and Other Silly Dilly Songs*. New York: Scholastic.

Lewis, J. Patrick. 2005. "Necessary Gardens," from *Please Bury Me in the Library*. San Diego, CA: Harcourt.

——. 2005. "Please Bury Me in the Library," from *Please Bury Me in the Library*. San Diego, CA: Harcourt.

Livingston, Myra Cohn. 1994. "Quiet" in Hopkins, Lee Bennett, selector. *April Bubbles Chocolate; An ABC of Poetry*. New York: Simon & Schuster.

Lottridge, Celia Barker. "Anna Marie's Library Book" and "What Happened," in Deborah Pearson, editor, *When I Went to the Library*. Toronto: Groundwood Books.

McLoughland, Beverly. 1990. "Surprise" in Hopkins, Lee Bennett. 1990. *Good Books, Good Times!* New York: HarperTrophy.

Medina, Jane. 1999. "The Library Card," from *My Name is Jorge on Both Sides of the River: Poems*. Honesdale, PA: Boyds Mills Press.

Merriam, Eve. 1998. "Reach for a Book," in Mary Perrotta Rich, editor, *Book Poems: Poems from National Children's Book Week, 1959–1998*. New York: Children's Book Council.

Nye, Naomi Shihab. 1998. "Because of Libraries We Can Say These Things," from *Fuel*. Rochester, NY: BOA Editions.

Prelutsky, Jack. 2006. "It's Library Time," from *What a Day It Was at School!* New York: Greenwillow.

Silverstein, Shel. 1981. "Overdues," from *A Light in the Attic*. New York: HarperCollins.

Soto, Gary. 1992. "Ode to My Library," from *Neighborhood Odes*. San Diego, CA: Harcourt.

Worth, Valerie. 1994. "Library," from *All the Small Poems and Fourteen More*. New York: Farrar, Straus & Giroux.

Based, in part, on: Vardell, S.M. 2006. A Place for Poetry: Celebrating the Library in Poetry. *Children and Libraries* 4(2): 35–41.

Poetry Practices Checklist

Consider these questions as you assess your poetry collection and common poetry practices:

✓ Are the poetry books as easy to find as the fiction and nonfiction?

✓ Are the poetry books in a child-friendly location, easily reachable, with the area well labeled and quickly identified?

✓ Do poetry posters and poetry book displays invite children to browse through poetry even if they're not immediately seeking it out?

✓ Are some poetry books displayed face out?

✓ Is there room on the poetry shelves for expansion?

✓ Are the poetry books on the shelf current?

✓ Is there a balance of poetry anthologies and collections by individual poets?

✓ Are the poetry award winners represented and highlighted?

✓ Are there multiple copies of the most current and popular poetry titles?

✓ Do you mention children's poetry choices when general subject requests come up?

✓ Do you include children's poetry books on your recommended reading lists and bibliographies?

✓ Do you actively seek out poetry books from diverse perspectives?

✓ Do you feature individual children's poets in displays, materials, and book talks?

✓ Do you incorporate poems for children alongside your story times and read alouds?

✓ Do you provide opportunities for children to participate actively in the choral reading performance of poetry?

✓ Do you have special plans for National Poetry Month and Young People's Poetry Week?

If we're serious about helping children discover poetry and then return to it again and again, we need to make this gem of the library obvious, easily reachable, and even unavoidable. One elementary school library media specialist noted an increase in poetry circulation after sharing a single poem with students each week as they entered the library, according to researchers Wilson and Kutiper in "Beyond Silverstein and Prelutsky: Enhancing and

Promoting the Elementary and Middle School Poetry Collection" published in *Youth Services in Libraries* in 1994. For a sampling of "welcome" poems to share, see the list of "Poems about Libraries and Reading" provided here.

References

The research tools for this project included the usual biographical reference works such as the *Something About the Author* series and Gale Databases such as Contemporary Authors Online and the Dictionary of Literary Biography. In addition, the Web sites of individual poets, when available, were consulted, as was the Web site for the Academy of American Poets. The following print resources were also extremely helpful.

Copeland, Jeffrey S. 1993. *Speaking of Poets: Interviews with Poets Who Write for Children and Young Adults.* Urbana, IL: National Council of Teachers of English.

Copeland, Jeffrey, S. and Copeland, Vicky S. 1995. *Speaking of Poets 2: More Interviews with Poets Who Write for Children and Young Adults.* Urbana, IL: National Council of Teachers of English.

Fox, Mem. 2001. *Reading Magic; Why Reading Aloud to Our Children Will Change Their Lives Forever.* San Diego, CA: Harcourt.

Hopkins, Lee Bennett. 1986. *Pass the Poetry Please.* 3rd edition. New York: HarperCollins.

——. 1995. *Pauses; Autobiographical Reflections of 101 Creators of Children's Books.* New York: HarperCollins.

Bibliography

Professional resources related to children's poetry:

Ada, Alma Flor, Harris, Violet, and Hopkins, Lee Bennett. 1993. *A Chorus of Cultures; Developing Literacy through Multicultural Poetry*. Carmel, CA: Hampton-Brown.

Barton, Bob and Booth, David. 2004. *Poetry Goes to School: From Mother Goose to Shel Silverstein*. Markham, ON: Pembroke Publishers.

Bauer, Caroline Feller. 1995. *The Poetry Break: An Annotated Anthology with Ideas for Introducing Children to Poetry*. New York: H. W. Wilson.

Booth, David and Moore, Bill. 2003. *Poems Please! Sharing Poetry with Children*. 2nd edition. Markham, ON: Pembroke Publishers.

Chatton, Barbara. 1993. *Using Poetry Across the Curriculum*. Phoenix, AZ: Oryx Press.

Cullinan, Bernice, Scala, Marilyn, and Schroder, Virginia. 1995. *Three Voices: An Invitation to Poetry Across the Curriculum*. York, ME: Stenhouse Publishers.

Heard, Georgia. 1994. *For the Good of the Earth and Sun; Teaching Poetry*. Portsmouth, NH: Heinemann.

——. 1999. *Awakening the Heart: Exploring Poetry in Elementary and Middle School*. Portsmouth, NH: Heinemann.

Holbrook, Sara. 2002. *Wham! It's a Poetry Jam: Discovering Performance Poetry*. Honesdale, PA: Wordsong/Boyds Mills Press.

——. 2005. *Practical Poetry: A Nonstandard Approach to Meeting Content-Area Standards*. Portsmouth, NH: Heinemann.

McClure, Amy. 1990. *Sunrises and Songs: Reading and Writing Poetry in the Classroom*. Portsmouth, NH: Heinemann.

Sloan, Glenna. 2003. *Give Them Poetry: A Guide for Sharing Poetry with Children K-8*. New York: Teachers College Press.

Steinbergh, Judith. 1994. *Reading and Writing Poetry: A Guide for Teachers*. New York: Scholastic.

Tiedt, Iris McLellan. 2002. *Tigers, Lilies, Toadstools, and Thunderbolts: Engaging K-8 Students with Poetry*. Newark, DE: International Reading Association.

Vardell, Sylvia M. 2006. *Poetry Aloud Here: Sharing Poetry with Children in the Library*. Chicago, IL: American Library Association.

About the Author

SYLVIA M. VARDELL is currently Professor at Texas Woman's University in the School of Library and Information Studies, where she teaches graduate courses in children's and young adult literature. She received her Ph.D. from the University of Minnesota in 1983. Vardell has published articles in *Book Links, Children and Libraries, School Library Journal, Language Arts, English Journal, The Reading Teacher, The New Advocate, Young Children, Social Education, and Horn Book,* as well as several chapters and books on language and literature, including *Poetry Aloud Here; Sharing Poetry with Children in the Library,* published by the American Library Association in 2006. Vardell helped establish the annual Texas Poetry Festival and organizes the "Poetry Round Up" session at the Texas Library Association conference, modeled after the ALSC Poetry Blast held at the annual ALA convention. She served on the National Council of Teachers of English committee that established the Orbis Pictus Award for Outstanding Nonfiction for Children and as co-chair of the NCTE Poetry Award committee. She has presented at many state, regional, national, and international conferences, and has received grants from the Middle East Policy Council, the Ezra Jack Keats Foundation, the National Council of Teachers of English, the ALAN Foundation, the Texas Library Association, HumanitiesTexas, and the National Endowment for the Humanities. She taught at the University of Zimbabwe in Africa as a Fulbright scholar in 1989. She is married, has two children, and is a naturalized American citizen.